# SUNRUNNERS ™

Let them hate. So long as they fear.
—Lucius Accius

# Credits

**Design:** M. Blaze Miskulin

**Additional Design Contributions:**
Donald Dennis, Tim Schmidt,
Heike A. Kubasch

**Cover Tradedress:** Nick Morawitz
**Cover Design:** Nick Morawitz
**Cover Illustration:** Kevin Ward
**Interior Illustration:** Dan Smith
**Miniatures Sculptor:** Bob Naismith
**Editor:** Donald (Walsfeo) Dennis
**Content Editor:** Bruce Neidlinger
**Art Direction:** Jessica Ney-Grimm
**Assistant Art Director:** Jason O. Hawkins
**Pagemaking:** Wendy Frazer
**Editorial Contributions:**
Heike A. Kubasch

ICE Staff:
*CEO:* Bruce Neidlinger;
*President:* Pete Fenlon;
*Managing Editor:* Coleman Charlton;
*Print buyer/Rights direction:* Kurt Fischer;
*Operations/Sales Manager:*
   Deane Begiebing;
*Sales, Customer Service, & Operations:*
   Olivia Johnston, Monica Wilson,
   Dave Platnick;
*Editing, Production and Development:*
   John Curtis, Donald G. Dennis,
   Wendy Frazer, Jason O. Hawkins,
   Nick Morawitz, Jessica Ney-Grimm,
Michael Reynolds;
*Shipping and Receiving:* Dave Morris,
   Daniel Williams.

# Silent Death

## Playtest Groups

*4 Horsemen:* Craig Marek, Doug Bertram, Bob Star, Kip Harris. *Players' Guild of Central Oklahoma:* John Foster, Roger Allen, Lisa Faran. *Rabid Wombats:* Stuart Templeton, Argon Smith, Kelly Rogers, Chris Henofer.

## Playtest forums

Rock Con, Soonercon, Hexacon, and the Pharaoh's Guard

# Contents

# Introduction

This is the Frontier.

It is a vast expanse of death, void, and rock, yet within its bounds lie the myriad worlds which were once the great Terran Empire. Most are now dead, stripped of their life by the swarming hordes of the Night Brood. Those who lived on these worlds have fled in the great arks, seeking a home safe from the destruction and horror. A few remain. Some hide quietly. Others prepare for war. The rest slowly die.

One of the suns which shines in the vastness of the Frontier is Barat-Gull, the center of what was the Barat Confederacy. On the capitol world Barat-Tuul, a colony of fierce warriors became a powerful state.

Barat-Tuul became the center of a vast and growing market for military starcraft and ordnance. The greatest weapons producer in the forward Frontier, they grew rich and powerful. In their power they grew proud; this was their downfall.

From their ruins were born the Sunrunners, a small ruthless band of mercenary warriors with the determination and ability to survive in what was left of the Frontier after the Terran-Hatchling War. With only their skills and the scattered remains of an empire-wide information net to work with, the small band slowly grew, becoming famous for both their warrior skills and their savage code of ethics.

## The Frontier

The Forward Frontier—the edge toward the direction of galactic spin—is the home of the Sunrunners. The Frontier was ravaged by the Hatchling swarms, and the Forward was no exception. Only about 1 world in 10 survived through the end of the war. Of those, even more fell to internal struggle or starvation in the years to follow. The planets that remained were the strongest, the smartest, or the luckiest.

Their luck, however, is running out fast. The strong and the smart are growing again, rebuilding what fell or starting fresh, and the new powers are not always the same as the old powers.

## Bethany

Bethany is a specialized agricultural world which is the main source of many medicines needed throughout the Forward Frontier. With the destruction of the Core and the fall of the Empire's vast trading routes, the Frontier areas have had to create their own sources for much of what was once freely available. Bethany rose in the post-war era to fill one such void. This small world has created a market for its drugs, both medical and recreational, in the Forward Frontier.

The Bethan are a peaceful people, but as has been proved in the past, have the ability to hold their own in a fire fight. Because of its economic power and the virtual monopoly it has on certain drugs, Bethany holds a large amount of sway in the political arena. Up to this point, however, the Bethans have chosen to stay out of the affairs of others, and have entered into no alliances. They are not, however, truly neutral. They have made the choice to not do business with certain societies and confederations (including the Draconians) and have shown special favor to others. All of this is done under the cover of business, and is kept away from the normal political channels.

## The Bokchito Collective

The Bokchito Collective is a rebuilt society of miners and manufacturers. At the height of the new Empire and through most of its waning years, the Bokchi planets were simply a source of raw materials for the Empire, and were held tightly under the Emperor's thumb. With the fall of the Empire, the Bokchi have come into their own. Fighting one of the most suc-

cessful holding actions against the Hatchlings, the Bokchi lost not a single planet to the Grubs. While the eradication of the Empire and the Core caused major problems with their economy, they had invested most of their money on their own worlds, and still retained it. That, along with a full system of planets clean of Grub infestation, was the boost which allowed them to not only resume their former power, but increase and refine it as well.

The mining of both the rock planets and gas giants continues uninterrupted, but the resources gathered now stay within the Collective. This has allowed them to build a sizable military. As yet, they have not advanced upon many other systems, being more interested in building the strength of their own worlds before taking others.

## Keota Enclave

Once a large and influential power in the Frontier, the Keota Enclave sustained heavy losses of both life and land in the War. They retreated from their outer worlds, and made a last stand on their capitol world of Keota. This happened at the end of the War, and luck was on their side. For whatever reasons, the Grubs left, content apparently with the several worlds they had claimed in the system. Fearing a return, the Keotans quickly began pooling their resources and built a small but adequate defense for their last world. After it was determined that the Hatchlings had gone into hibernation, the Keotans started to slowly and quietly rebuild what was left of their society.

The Keotans are a technological people, known for their exquisite (and often esoteric) machines and ideas. Much of what they produce is in the form of computations only, and seems to have little to do with the physical universe. They have, however, come up with a few ideas that others have found useful. Their power in the frontier is almost entirely due to their technology. They have very little in the way of a military, and no materials worth selling. They trade in information. Most of the Frontier worlds simply let the Keotans tinker and think, not feeling threatened by them or needing their help. This situation suits the Keotans just fine.

## Prague

Once a holding of the Bokchi, Prague is one of the new powers for whom the infiltration by the Grubs was advantageous. Left to its own defenses by the Bokchi, Prague took a strong economy and turned it to the production of weapons and training of soldiers. Having been a major arms manufacturer in the past, this took little effort.

With the end of the War, Prague began to use its new-found power to advance upon its neighbors. Soon what was once a single system became a collection. Prague no longer has to worry about being swallowed up by the larger powers. Instead, it has become a major contender in the race for supremacy in the frontier.

## Rattan

Rattan is perhaps the most powerful foward frontier society to survive the War. Quick to take advantage of the post-War chaos, the Rattanni quickly grew to replace the worlds they sacrificed during the War. They are a ruthless and domineering culture, strong in their military and their politics. The calm and peaceful society that is shown to the rest of the frontier is kept that way by subjugation of the masses by the militaristic government. The Rattanni hierarchy cares little for the lower classes and, as has been shown in the past, is willing to sacrifice them if it suits their needs. Through the diligent use of propaganda, the careful gathering of information and the open show of force, the Rattanni keep their subjugated planets in line. Through these techniques, Rattan has been able to get incredible amounts of work out of its people. Most of this work has been focused on the growth of its military and the conquest of new worlds.

The major adversary in the continued growth of Rattan is Bokchito. The Rattanni leaders are unwilling to engage in open hostilities with the Bokchi, knowing that to do so would instigate a large-scale war. Instead, each tries to corrupt the other from within. So far, this has done little except keep the propagandists in business.

The remainder of the Frontier is comprised of single worlds, small confederations and outposts. There is, however, one strong power in the Frontier that everyone must contend with.

## Pirates

When the Hatchling swarms scoured the Frontier planets, they killed and displaced billions of people. Of those who fled their homes, most took to the great arks in search of worlds free from the Hatchling horror. Some, however, remained within their old territories as free-roaming bands of pirates. The majority of these are former fighter wings from powerful planets or remnants of the Imperial Navy. Some have retained their names and even designations, even though the worlds they report to be from may no longer exist.

These pirates are bands ranging in size from a few small ships to entire wings supported by carriers. Most have found some small asteroid or abandoned outpost to claim as their new home, often at the cost of the former inhabitants' lives, and use that as a base to work from. This has caused a certain amount of territorial ranging. The pirates stay close to the worlds they came from—the areas they know well.

The major exception to this are the Imperial remnants. These are wings of the former Imperial Navy, who deserted during the war or were trapped in the Frontier until the War's conclusion. The remnants are considered to be the fiercest of the pirates, and the most unpredictable. They tend to have better equipment and better crews than other pirates, and have no set territory. There is growing suspicion that the Imperial remnants may be secretly supported by the Twelve in an effort to keep the Frontier unions from growing in power. Even the large unions such as Bokchito and Rattan are not free from the pickings of the pirates.

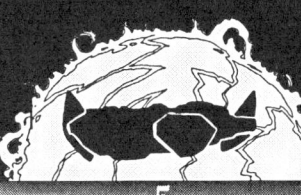

# Worlds of the Forward Frontier

For more detailed information on habitable worlds see *Appendix A (p.75-79)*.

## System Listings

The following pieces describe each of Espan's star systems. Each system is rendered as an easy-to-read graphic. The stars are labeled by spectral class (A-S), relative temperature (0-9) and stellar type (i-v). Planets and asteroid belts are depicted in their orbits' order and are labeled by type:

⊗ - A planet that has a solid mantle of rock. The planet's environment may vary from habitable to non-existent.

● - A gas giant, typically a celestial mass of various gases that with a bit more mass may have become a small star.

∴ - Asteroid belt, This is an area of celestial debris, in some cases it may be material that never collected together to form a planet or an errant moon that was torn asunder by the gravitational flux of the other planets.

| PLANETARY KEY | | | |
|---|---|---|---|
| | ∴ | ● | ⊗ |
| # | Belt width (km) | diameter (km) | diameter(km) |
| 0 | 10000-20000 | 30000-40000 | 1-1000 |
| 1 | 20001-30000 | 40001-50000 | 1001-2000 |
| 2 | 30001-40000 | 50001-60000 | 2001-3000 |
| 3 | 40001-50000 | 60001-70000 | 3001-4000 |
| 4 | 50001-70000 | 70001-80000 | 4001-5000 |
| 5 | 70001-90000 | 80001-90000 | 5001-6000 |
| 6 | 90001-120000 | 90001-100000 | 6001-7000 |
| 7 | 120001-150000 | 100001-110000 | 7001-8000 |
| 8 | 150001-200000 | 110001-125000 | 8001-9000 |
| 9 | 200001-300000 | 125001-150000 | 9001-10000 |

**System:** Ares
**Habitable Worlds:** V (primary moon)
**Resource Worlds:** VII, X
**Notes:** Ares is a minor manufacturing state in the frontier. They are primarily involved with the milling of precision gauges.

**System:** Argent
**Habitable Worlds:** III, VI
**Resource Worlds:** I, V, VII-IX
**Notes:** A rather old and minor power in the frontier, Argent gained new vigor in the post-War years. It is mineral-rich but agriculture poor. It is in constant need of agricultural resources.

**System:** PKF-7981
**Habitable Worlds:** Athenia (I)
**Resource Worlds:** None
**Notes:** Athenia is a minor world with no importance except for its location.

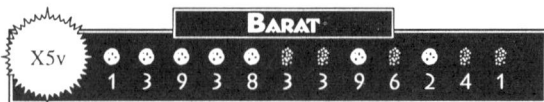

**System:** Barat
**Habitable Worlds:** Barat-Tuul (III), Barat-Shan (IV)
**Resource Worlds:**
**Notes:** Formerly an industrial and mining conglomerate, the planets of the Barat system are now heavily infested with Hatchlings.

| X3v | ● | ●● | ●● | ●● | ● |
|---|---|---|---|---|---|
| | 9 | 4 | 9 | 2 | 5 |

**System:** Beta 795
**Habitable Worlds:** Bethany (III)
**Resource Worlds:** None
**Notes:** Bethany is a major pharmaceutical producer in the forward frontier. It's population is over 80% female.

| X4v | ● | ●● | ●● | ●● | ● | ●● | ● |
|---|---|---|---|---|---|---|---|
| | 5 | 5 | 8 | 0 | 7 | 3 | 5 |

**System:** Bokchito
**Habitable Worlds:** Bokchito III, IV, VI
**Resource Worlds:** I-VII
**Notes:** Bokchito is a mineral-rich system, and is heavily industrialized and militarized.

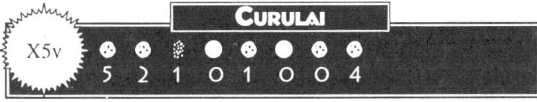

| X5v | ● | ●● | ● | ● | ●● | ● | ●● | ● |
|---|---|---|---|---|---|---|---|---|
| | 5 | 2 | 1 | 0 | 1 | 0 | 0 | 4 |

**System:** Curulai
**Habitable Worlds:** Kayan (III), Raash (IV)
**Resource Worlds:** II, V, VI
**Notes:** The Curulai are small, peaceful worlds which trade in rare trace minerals and heavy metals. They have very little industry and very little military.

| X3v | ●● | ●● | ●● | ●● | ● |
|---|---|---|---|---|---|
| | 1 | 8 | 8 | 4 | 6 |

**System:** KZ-24N9
**Habitable Worlds:** Homestead (II)
**Resource Worlds:** Sutter's Rock (secondary moon of KZ-24N9/V)
**Notes:** Homestead is a small agricultural colony of little significance except as a food producer.

| X6v | ●● | ● | ●● | ● | ● | ●● | ● | ●● | ●● | ●● | ● |
|---|---|---|---|---|---|---|---|---|---|---|---|
| | 2 | 1 | 4 | 9 | 6 | 7 | 8 | 4 | 6 | 2 2 | 5 |

**System:** Kernat
**Habitable Worlds:** Kernat III, IV (Keota), VI, IX
**Resource Worlds:** Kernat I, XII
**Notes:** Keota is the last remaining planet of the Kernat system which is free of Hatchling infestation. The Keotan society is based on technological superiority, and is considered eccentric by outsiders.

**Silent Death**

X5v · 6 4 6 4 1 6 9 3

**System:** Prague
**Habitable Worlds:** II, IV (satellite 4),
    IV (satellite 6)
**Resource Worlds:** IV (satellite 3),
    VI (satellite 3), VII, VIII
**Notes:** Prague is a an old government
    which has found new power after be-
    ing released from the domination of the
    Bokchi government. In the post-War
    years, it has used it's new strength to
    expand into the surrounding space.

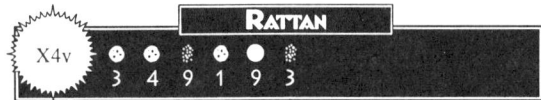

X4v · 3 4 9 1 9 3

**System:** Rattan
**Habitable Worlds:** II, IV
**Resource Worlds:** V (satellite 3), VI
**Notes:** Rattan is a heavily populated and
    overtaxed system with real need for ex-
    pansion.

X4v · 3 8 3 4

**System:** Taber
**Habitable Worlds:** II
**Resource Worlds:** III, IV (primary satellite)
**Notes:** Taber is a new minor power looking
    for a military buffer in case of Grub re-
    turn.

X3v · 9 1 4 6 9

**System:** Vian
**Habitable Worlds:** IV (Vian)
**Resource Worlds:** IV
**Notes:** Vian is a religious colony of Bhuddist
    monks. Planetary conditions are rough,
    but the large gemstone wealth is prof-
    itable for those who can survive.

X2v · 5 4 8

**System:** Wann
**Habitable Worlds:** Wann (I)
**Resource Worlds:** III (secondary moon)
**Notes:** Though severely damaged in the
    War, Wann survived as a collection of
    outlaws and political bullies who have
    formed a cohesive government—of
    sorts. They aggressively defend their
    territory and are adamant about oth-
    ers upholding treaties.

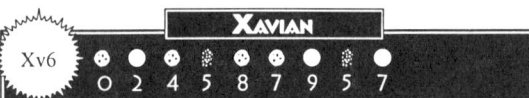

Xv6 · 0 2 4 5 8 7 9 5 7

**System:** Xavian
**Habitable Worlds:** Xavian V
**Resource Worlds:** III
**Notes:** Xavian is an isolationist planet of
    little interest to the larger powers of the
    frontier. It is, however, often a favored
    target of pirates.

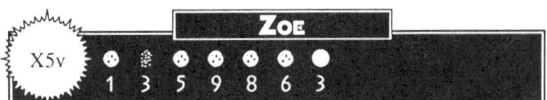

X5v · 1 3 5 9 8 6 3

**System:** Kursh
**Habitable Worlds:** Zoe (IV)
**Resource Worlds:** I, II
**Notes:** Zoe was destroyed by Grub infesta-
    tion, and its survivors fled.

# Sunrunners

The last power of note in the frontier is the Sunrunners. The only remaining survivors of Barat-Tuul, they have formed a free-roaming band of mercenaries who are famous throughout the frontier and most of the former Empire as some of the best in the business.

The destruction of Barat-Tuul heralded the beginning of the end of the Terran Empire. As the strength of the Emperor diminished and his power concentrated on keeping himself and his Empire alive, the smaller houses and factions of the frontier took advantage of the situation. What had been carefully controlled skirmishes in the past now grew into large battles and full-scale wars between planets and systems. With the increase in the hostilities came the waking of the Night Brood.

Still unaware of the reason for the Hatchling incursions, the frontier planets began scaling up their wars to include the Grubs. The balances and lines of power shifted daily, and common soldiers were unsure, from day to day, just who was an enemy and who was an ally.

In the midst of all this chaos, several of the noncombatants became unwitting victims. The Grubs cared little for which planets wakened them, and simply eradicated everyone and everything in their path. It was a situation such as this which befell the populace of Barat-Tuul.

Because of their valuable position—supplying ships and ordnance to any and all who had the money or trade to purchase—the Barat were secure in their safety from attack. In addition, there was an unwritten understanding among their clients that any agency that did attack Barat-Tuul would face retribution not only from the Barat themselves, but from any and all forces doing business with them.

It was this secure position that proved to be their downfall. In knowing that no force would be willing to face the consequences of attacking the Barat, they kept a relatively minor defensive force in the system, sending many of their viable fighter units out to neighboring systems to train and work as mercenaries. When the Night Brood invasion started, the planet was poorly defended, and quickly lost its forces to the unfamiliar ships and tactics of the Grubs. (While the Barat were known as exceptional fighters, it was generally accepted that they had a weakness in their adaptive strategic abilities.) An all-call went out to the rest of the fighter wings throughout the surrounding sectors, and each headed homeward at top speed. Unfortunately, due to the disruption of communications, it was impossible to organize this mass return, and the wings arrived, a few at a time, and were easily destroyed by the now firmly entrenched Grubs.

The last to return were four carriers conducting extended maneuvers deep in unclaimed territories: the *Maelstrom*, *Huntress*, *Vulcan*, and *Crescent Moon*. While each of these carriers was considered an independent force, the other three deferred to the seniority of Admiral Michael "Odin" Bach aboard the *Maelstrom*. Bach had a reputation of strength and ferocity that few among the ranks dared to challenge—including the other captains.

The last four carriers, low on supplies, launched all they had against the Grubs in a vain attempt to wipe them from the skies above Barat-Tuul. As with the earlier attempts, they failed.

## Good Business

The Sunrunners have a standing policy: Grubs are free. Any Hatchlings will be battled by any Sunrunner force, regardless of who is being defended, for no fee. If the defended colony wishes, it may replace spent ammunition, but this is by no means required or even expected of them. The Sunrunners' hatred for the Grubs is such that any chance to exterminate a few more is taken as a gift. This policy has helped their reputation immensely, and gained them favor of some powerful nations.

Admiral. Admiral!" The voice of the communications officer filtered through the noise of the party. "Admiral."

"Hey, Regin. What can I do for you?" Admiral Bach turned to the young man beside him, at last acknowledging his calls.

"Sir. We have a small problem. You're requested to return to the bridge right away, sir."

"For the love of the Gods." He took a long last drink from the tankard in front of him and slammed it back down on the table. He dragged his shirt sleeve across his thickly bearded face, soaking up the ale foam before standing and pulling his uniform jacket off his chair's back and walking solidly out of the room and towards the bridge.

"Son, this had better be important. I don't appreciate having my drinking interrupted. This is the last time I'll be having a return party, and I want to make the most of it." With a push from his mighty arm, the hatch to the bridge swung open, and Admiral Michael "Odin" Bach strode in. "So what in the nine hells is going on that you can't handle by yourselves?"

"Sir." Bach turned to the familiar voice at his right. The man it came from stood tall and proud, looking the Admiral squarely in the eye—a significant feat considering the Admiral's size. The two men were cast from the same mold, though the younger man's sizable mass was still tight with youth, while the Admiral's had smoothed slightly with age. They were, in fact, father and son, the younger being Tomass, captain of the Maelstrom, though he was known more widely as Thor—a nickname he did nothing to discourage.

He and his father had earned their names while defending a mining operation against insurgents. Out of ammo, the two held a key passage in the mine by fighting hand to hand, Tomass swinging one of the heavy sledges used to break the hard stones. The sound of their fierce battle cries and the thundering slam of the hammer echoed throughout the mine and hung in their enemies' memories long after the two defenders emerged from the deep shaft, covered in the blood of their attackers, the deadly hammer still gripped in Tomass' hand. The mythical image could not be ignored.

Now the two of them stood facing each other on the bridge of the carrier Maelstrom. "It's Barat-Tuul. They're sending a distress call."

"What city?"

"No city. The whole planet."

"What?"

"Grubs."

"DAMN!" The Admiral's fist slammed into the wall beside him, just missing a bank of display screens. "Can we get there in time to do anything?"

"No."

Michael looked at his son with his one good eye, his left thumb absently scratching at the patch which covered the other. With a jerk he pulled the hand away and stood straight. "Do it anyway."

"Yes, sir!"

\* \* \*

"All ships ready to fly. The Huntress, Vulcan, and Crescent Moon report same. 2 minutes to jump-down."

"Any word from Barat-Tuul?"

"Nothing, sir. Just dead air."

"The air may be the only thing that's left alive, boy, don't kill it too." Admiral Bach stood looking out the front screen of the bridge. He'd heard tales of what the Night Brood could do to a world; now they were on his. No response came from the planet. Four billion people, and no one was able to reach a com station. Were the four carriers under his command the last? Less than five hundred active ships with limited crews to staff them. "For their sakes, let's hope the Valkyrie are well rested. They'll have their work cut out for them today."

"Pardon me, sir?"

"Nothing, Ensign." He took one last look at the screen and turned his attention back to his crew. "Noggins, any luck sorting out the scanners?"

"None, sir. There's too much debris. I can't tell what's an active ship and what's scrap metal."

"Thirty seconds to jump-down, sir."

"Sound the alert. Regin, I want constant reports from the other three carriers."

"Twenty seconds."

"All pilots! Prepare to launch." The Admiral's formidable voice dropped to a cold growl. "Kill 'em, kids. Let 'em know we're here."

"Ten seconds." Despite the flurry of activity, the bridge seemed unnaturally quiet as all eyes looked to the forward screen.

"Jump-down." The carriers broke into normal space just outside Barat-Tuul's orbit, letting the fighters launch at high velocities before reducing speed to within the system's safety limits.

"All fighters launched, sir."

Within a few short minutes, the vast black sky in front of them began to light up, small stars flashing into existence for

a brief second, then fading into the void, with no voice to tell if they were man or monster.

For almost an hour, Bach watched the screen, listening to the sporadic reports delivered by his bridge crew, watching the tiny stars erupt with death in the silence.

"Regin."

"Yes, sir?"

"Put the fighter band on line. I want to hear what's going on out there."

"Yes, sir." The young man turned back to his post and flipped a small switch to his right.

"—IT! Repeat: I'm hit! Pulling back—"

"Mighty Mother of the Gods! IT'S—

"—ay with your wing!"

"Too late, she's breaking up—"

"—ave destroyed. Hang on, we'll be—"

"Die, you bastard! DIE!"

Admiral Bach continued to listen to the shouts of his pilots as they flew against wave after wave of the alien ships. As the minutes passed, often-heard voices fell silent, and those that still spoke did so with growing strain.

"Regin." The Admiral remained facing the front screen, but his quieted voice still reached the communications officer. "Sound the recall."

"Admiral?"

"Sound the recall."

"But, sir..."

"Get those men out of there!" His voice thundered through the room, echoing off the metal walls. All eyes turned to the Admiral as the young officer behind him sounded the retreat.

\* \* \*

In an unprecedented action, Admiral Michael Bach pulled the forces under his command back to a safe distance, to regroup and flee if necessary. This was all that saved them.

At the point that Admiral Michael Bach ordered the retreat of the fighter forces, they had been decimated. Out of the original 500 fighters, barely 200 were left, and most of those were in no condition to fight. The pilots were no better. Lacking the needed medical facilities, dozens more of the pilots died in the following few days. Even then, it almost ended with a mutiny and subsequent return to battle against the Hatchlings. Admiral Bach, however, had

# Silent Death

## Mimir

The Sunrunner intelligence network—the last remnant of Barat-Tuul's former power—is known as Mimir. In the legends of their ancestors, is the tale of the great sage Mimir, who's severed head was sent by the enemies of Asgard to Odin's hall as a sign of their hatred. Odin took this severed head and rubbed it with magical oils and fragrant herbs, bringing it back to a semblance of life. Untroubled by the lack of a body, Mimir continued to provide sage advice to the leader of the gods.

*the strength of will to maintain his command and turn the remnants of his wings into a viable fighting force with a long-term goal.*

*Admiral Bach ordered the remains of the Barat-Tuul fleet to retreat to outside the system. This was the move that almost precipitated a mutiny from the outraged pilots and crews. Never before had the warriors of Barat-Tuul fled from an enemy force. Despite his personal opinions, Tomass Bach stood with his father and, in doing so, kept the fleet together. No one was willing to stand against the two men.*

\* \* \*

The people of Barat-Tuul were descended from a long line of warriors and, indeed, prided themselves on their ability in this area. They had remained outside of the power struggles which surrounded them. Instead, they became one of the major producers of fighter craft and ordnance for the sector. Their production of small craft, which matched and, in some cases, surpassed the Imperial fighter craft, was a boon to the smaller houses and factions who could not afford to pay black-market prices for Pit Vipers or Imperial craft.

Sitting in the center of a mineral-rich system, Barat-Tuul could produce both ships and weapons at relatively cheap prices and, because of the short delivery distances to the combatants, offer even greater discounts. Despite all this, they could still leave an impressive mark-up on their products and became extremely wealthy in their own right.

In addition to supplying the ships and weapons, the Barat-Tuul also supplied warriors—pilots, gunners, and technicians—to train the purchasing armies in the use of the somewhat unusual and occasionally unorthodox equipment. The Barat were known throughout the surrounding sectors as the best fighter pilots alive.

The last nail in the coffin of Barat was the pride of its people. Most of the Barat warriors never considered retreating, preferring to die in the attempt to retake their planet. They did just that.

\* \* \*

*"How many fighters do we have left?"*

*"Two hundred and six." Captain Terri Hawking of the Huntress looked despairingly at Admiral Bach. "Twenty nine of those will barely make it out of the launch bay—if that. Of the remainder, only about a hundred are in any shape to fight."*

*"And that's assuming we could find fuel and armaments." Willem Gold of the Crescent Moon had the same look of defeat on his face. "We'll be lucky if we can arm a dozen of those fighters."*

*The last captain, Gregor Jensson of the Vulcan, simply sat with his hands on his lap, his face unreadable behind its thick beard.*

"So," Admiral Bach turned where he was standing and stared at the blank wall beside him. "If we return and try to fight, we will die. Uselessly." He turned back to the other captains, his single eye looking from one to the other, "I will not send these men back to die. You all know me. You know I do not fear what they may do to me, or to my men," Behind its patch the muscles of his missing eye twitched briefly, "But I will not walk blindly to my death, either. I don't want funerals, I want answers."

"We do have friends."

"Friends that will fight against Grubs, Terri? I think their friendship will extend only so far."

"Come on, Michael. At the very least, let's see what we can get. I'm not too proud to beg."

"I am." Bach stared directly at the woman, his cold pride showing. "And so are my warriors." He added a stress to that last word.

"If I may?" Gregor finally spoke, his voice quiet and sure. "I, also, am too proud to beg, but I am not too proud to bargain. We have alliances. Use them. Let us get what we can and move on."

"You may be right. Terri, if you were to use some of the other ships for spare parts, how many viable fighters could you give me?"

"I might me able to bring the number up to 150. But as Willem said, we only have torps for about a dozen."

"Steal cannons off ships with extras—whatever it takes. I want a fighting force of 150 ships. If it comes to a real fight, we'll throw stones if we have to. For now, let's let our reputation do some of the work for us." Bach smiled sinisterly. "It's much easier to win when the enemy is too scared to fight."

\* \* \*

"Admiral Bach to the flight deck, please. Admiral Bach to the flight deck." The call sounded through the intercom system of the large carrier catching the imposing man at his dinner.

"Damn." The quiet mutter had become familiar to the crew in the past few days. They no longer paid much attention to it, knowing that, invariably, whatever problem was important enough to interrupt the Admiral, would soon be solved to their advantage.

The large man shoved one last forkful of food into his mouth and, wiping the drippings out of his white beard, headed out of the mess hall and toward the flight deck, grumbling the entire time. The interruption didn't annoy him that much—he had become used to them lately—but he had found that a frequent dose of grumbling mixed with an occasional growl gave the crew the impression that he was constantly engaged in some important business on their behalf. It also caused them to move out of his way as he strode through the halls. This last, he found, was far more pleasing than the peace of mind of his crew.

"This had better be good. Once again you managed to catch me in the middle of my meal."

"Um...Sorry, sir." The chief technician looked around nervously, not wanting to be the victim of his Admiral's wrath.

"Well?"

"Over here, Michael." Bach looked behind the scared technician to see Terri Hawking step out from behind a pockmarked Havok. "You asked for viable fighters; I'm giving you viable fighters." The thick eyebrow over Bach's good eye rose questioningly. "It's only a hundred forty two, and they're stripped pretty bare, but they can fly, and they can fight."

"How bare?"

"No ship has more than one gun per gunner. In anything with more than one crew member, we took off the pilot's gun and mounted it where it could be better used. But we did make a few adjustments to offset it. I'd rather not take on the Grubs with these things, but we've got enough to make a few politicos believe we mean business."

Bach walked quietly along the line of fighters, giving a quick glance at each and making indeterminate grumbles just loud enough for those nearby to hear. "I thought you said we only had enough torps for a dozen ships. Over half of these ships are mounted with them." He turned to the Huntress's captain, "Dummies?"

"Nope. Something new. Hessler over there came up with it." She gestured at the now calmer chief technician. "You said you'd be willing to throw stones at the enemy if needed, so that's what we gave you."

# Silent Death

## The Ravens

Within the Mimir—the Sunrunner's intelligence network— are the Ravens. Two special forces of operatives known only as Hunin and Mugin—thought and memory. These two sections each have their areas of operation within the greater intelligence network. Hunin is thought. He takes new information or active information to and from the hidden bases and roaming carriers. Mugin is memory. He takes duplicate information and inactive information between the carriers and the bases to insure the redundancy of information.

The operatives of the two forces are specially equipped for their tasks. The largest of their tools are the specially prepared Windjammers. Painted matte-black and identified only with a single logo of gloss black,

*Again Bach's eyebrow rose questioningly, only this time accompanied by a scowl.*

*"We took the functional warheads of the torps we had and divided them among the loads of empty casings laying around. The remainder of the warhead space is filled with pieces from ruined ships. Detonate one of these things in front of a fighter doing a high velocity, and it's like flying through a meteor shower. We left a few torps untouched. The bad guys won't know which is which."*

*Bach grumbled some more, but nodded his head approvingly. "You've done the same thing with the rest of the fighters on the other carriers?"*

*"One hundred and forty-two fighters total. Yours were the last."*

*"Then let's get moving. If we don't find a place to restock the food, I'm going to start to get rather...disagreeable."*

\* \* \*

The gamble paid off. Retreating from their home, the four carriers began a systematic sweep of the surrounding sector, approaching allies and business partners.

Slowly, world by world, the Barat worked their way through the frontier, getting what they could from each of the governments they had dealt with in the past. Unwilling to show weakness by asking for help gratis, the Barat traded knowledge, skills, and salvage for new fuel and parts for the small fleet of fighters they had remaining. Among the trades was one which handed over the production designs for some of the Coring fighter craft in exchange for the process and facilities needed to produce the now-stable andrite. The *Crescent Moon* was converted over for this purpose and became almost exclusively an andrite production facility.

The other commodity the Barat were able to sell was information. During their years of business, they had developed one of the largest and most intricate private intelligence systems in the forward frontier. With the carefully rationed dispersal of important information, they were able to trade for more of the needed supplies.

Life aboard the carriers began to settle in. Knowing it would be years, if not generations, before they would have the strength to realize their goal of retaking their homeworld, the Barat slowly converted to a life of constant roaming. But those who had won the battles to save their homes began to look down on those who had lost theirs. The Barat took the brunt of this derision because, unlike others, they remained within the frontier and inner systems, refusing to search out a new world and new life. Their continual running from sun to sun was a constant reminder of the homeless on the surfaces of many planets. The term sunrunner became a general insult akin to "bum". That, however, would eventually change—with a little help from the Barat.

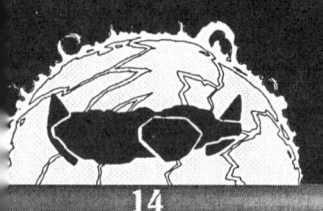

The careful building-up of the Barat forces to a self-sustaining condition took several years, during which the final battles in the Imperial Core and the great battles with the Grubs came into full swing. Admiral Bach saw this chaos as an opportunity, and he began to use the reputation of Barat warriors to their advantage. Now referring to themselves as the Sunrunners, the men and women of the three unmodified carriers began to sell their services to any who would buy. At first, they charged standard mercenary rates, using the cash to maintain their small fleet. Soon, however, Tomass Bach created the idea that became the modern Sunrunners.

Already, the Sunrunners had made a name for themselves in the rapidly disintegrating Empire as some of the best and most ruthless warriors to be bought. Bach decided to capitalize on that growing reputation and, at the same time, build a greater fighting force. With their admiral's approval, the Sunrunners began taking the jobs that other mercenaries wouldn't touch. They made a point of using wild and dangerous tactics and being ruthless in the pursuit and destruction of their foes. At the same time, they instituted a new policy for payment: salvage and bonus. They got paid for the ships they faced, and kept all salvage for themselves.

Soon the fleet grew. The *Crescent Moon* was dispatched from the other carriers with a small guard of fighters to search out suitable planets or other bodies on which to start up facilities for ship and weapon production. The remaining carriers each acted separately, meeting occasionally to restock and swap spare parts, extra craft and crew. Through selective recruitment and an aggressive birthing policy, the ranks grew to fill the available ships.

Many of the Sunrunners that exist today have been trained from birth to be warriors, and know no other life. Born and bred on the carriers to a nomadic life far from any home, many of those who now fight in the hopes of one day reclaiming Barat-Tuul, have never seen the planet. Despite a history of prejudice against their nomadic lifestyle, they are still some of the best mercenaries in the galaxy and are highly sought-after for their services.

\* \* \*

*Tomass walked quietly onto the bridge, leaned against the map display, his arms crossed casually across his chest, and looked at his father, a scowl of curiosity creasing his forehead. For over a minute he simply stood there.*

*"What in the nine hells are you looking at?" Michael spun from where he was reading the displays to stare back at his son.*

*"Your head."*

*"My head?"*

*"Yes."*

*"And why are you looking at my head?"*

*"I'm trying to figure out what's so special about it." For several seconds the admiral stood silent, unsure of how to respond. "It's not even that good of a head," Tomass continued. "It's old, rather ugly, and it's even missing pieces—and I must say, that WAS rather careless of you. Where as my head...well, now there's a work of art: handsome, strong, mature—yet young—and with all of it's fine pieces intact and in perfect working order."*

*"I will ask only once. Why this sudden interest in the condition of my head?"*

*"It seems the Emperor is rather taken with our heads. He wants them for himself. And for some reason he's willing to pay twice as much for yours as he is for mine. Maybe it has value as an antique."*

*A look of exasperation crossed over Michael's face and melted into a familiar scowl. "Apparently the Emperor realizes that my head has something inside of it, while yours would be good for little else than a jewel box. Now get the hell out and let me get something accomplished here." Tomass shrugged and casually walked towards the door. "Hold on a second."*

*"Yes, oh wise and aged father?"*

*"How much is he willing to pay for this ugly old head of mine?"*

*"500 k."*

*The admiral's chest began to shake, and his face twitched as a laugh began to work its way out of him. "Hah Hah! Tomass, my boy, it seems we're doing something right after all."*

\* \* \*

Because of their position in several of the instrumental battles close to the core, the Emperor outlawed the Sunrunners and put a sizable price on their heads. Being decreed outlaws was a major boost to the

they are virtually invisible in the darkness of space. Any information traveling solely by way of the Ravens is sent three times, with each ship traveling a different route.

# Silent Death

## Steeped in Legend

Though the Sunrunners do not all believe in the ancient gods of the Aesir as do the members of the Siguard Archdiocese, they do have strong ties to their Norse and Germanic heritage. This is shown in their tendency to use the names and traditions of their ancestors. They now refer to the planet of their origin as Niflheim—the land of the dead. Secret communications with their hidden bases are said to be sent by the ravens Hugin and Munin—thought and memory—the familiars of the ancient god Odin. And the flagship which shall eventually lead them to reclaim their lost world shall be known by the name Naglfar—the ship built by the queen of Hel from the fingernails of dead soldiers.

reputation of the Sunrunners. They took the pronouncement to heart, and adopted the attitude that, since they are outlaws, the laws do not apply to them. They are willing to use outlawed weapons (though they still refrain from anything that would wake a Clutch) and outlawed technology. They also disregard all boundaries and subscribe to no prescribed rules of war but their own.

With the Empire gone, the majority of the Twelve still hold that bounty in place. With little known to the outside about their true goals and policies, the Sunrunners are seen as a potential threat to the security of the Twelve, and a possible rival for territory and influence. In reality, the Sunrunners stay primarily in the frontier and outer provinces, and have no desire for any land or political power which would conflict with the interests of the Twelve. Viewing any unknown commodity as a potential threat, however, the Twelve maintain the decree of the Sunrunners as an outlaw organization. Two which hold exception to this ban are the Kashmere Commonwealth and the Sidgurd Archdiocese.

In their dealings in the Frontier, the Kashmere have found that the Sunrunners are a powerful ally. In many areas, the simple knowledge that the Sunrunners have extended their protection to the Kashmere is enough to prevent would-be attackers from attempting a raid—the

threat of combined retaliation by the two powers is a powerful deterrent. In the other direction, Kashmere is the single largest purchaser of scrap from the Sunrunners, an arrangement which is beneficial to both sides.

Among the Sunrunner's closest "ally" is the Sidgurd Archdiocese. Admiral Michael Bach shared many of the Midguardian beliefs even before the first Nightbrood swarmed. With the loss of Barat-Tuul, Midguardian clerics were welcomed aboard Sunrunner carriers to provide comfort and spiritual guidance to the grieving survivors. The Midguardian missionaries enthusiastically and competently fought beside the Sunrunners. Their missionary "fervor" won them many converts among the Barat. Admiral Bach, however, is too politic to make the worship of Odin the official faith of the Sunrunners. The arrival of the Promethians has strengthened the bond between the Sunrunners and the Archdiocese, since both fear and distrust aliens. The Archdiocese has representatives on all of the major Sunrunner ships, including the Crescent Moon.

One other among the Twelve has had dealings with the Sunrunners. House Red Star has been hired by the Sunrunners to do some minor terraforming, and has sold them some information on terraforming techniques for certain situations. Officially, House Red Star still considers the

Sunrunners to be outlaws, but in practical terms, economic necessity has prompted them to ignore the decree on occasion.

The Yoka-Shan have long despised the Sunrunners, even before the coming of the hatchlings. The Yoka-Shan fight for justice, the Sunrunners for money. In the eyes of the Yoka-Shan, the Sunrunners are no better than hired killers, and it was the Yoka-Shan who first dubbed the surviving Barat "Sunrunners." The loss of Barat-Tuul only increased the scorn of the Yoka-Shan, for they could feel no pity for the well-armed warriors who so carelessly lost their home world. Perhaps the scorn may one day give way to grudging respect when the two forces finally meet in battle, but to date the vast distances of Terran space have kept the foes apart.

The Sunrunners distrust the Primates and the Draconians equally. They have even accused the Promethians of deliberately setting the Brood on the Terran Empire in hopes of weakening and then dominating the human race. If there is one thing that the Primates and the Draconians have ever agreed upon, it is that the Sunrunner's suspicions are absurd. Now if the Draconians could find some way of controlling Grubs....

# Sunrunners Now

While their reputation may have spread throughout the reaches of Terran space, the Sunrunners themselves usually remain within the Frontier, and mostly the Forward at that. Yet even within that space, there is more than enough to keep the three wings of fighters busy. The various planets and unions of the Frontier are in a constant state of armed aggression. It seems that even after a war that destroyed the entire Core, the nature of Terrans is to fight. In this, the Sunrunners are at home. They have turned the business of war into a profitable one.

The Sunrunners have little voice as a political power, though they are respected as an independent state. The real power of the Sunrunners comes from their access to information. The intelligence network built up by the Barat and continued by the Sunrunners is one of the largest and most intricate available to a private organization. They have connections among most of the Twelve and virtually all of the Frontier planets. The one factor that has let them create such a complex network is its non-expansionist nature. Despite the suspicions of the Twelve, the Sunrunners are at war with no Terran government, and have no intention of being so at anytime in the future.

For the most part, the Sunrunners are highly isolationist, staying out of the political arena all together. On the rare incident when they have been forced into a political situation, they did so only to preserve their status, and then did only what was needed. They much prefer to settle business with a blaster.

No one knows for sure just how large the full Sunrunner force is. All that is ever seen of it are the three carriers and their contingent wings. On occasion, the fourth carrier, the *Crescent Moon*, has been seen in tandem with one of the other carriers. It is known that the Sunrunner fighting force is backed up by a large scientific community and a manufacturing base capable of supplying replacement starcraft while putting many of the same on the open market as well. There are also rumors throughout the frontier and inner reaches that there may be as many as five other carriers under construction, along with the fighters needed to fill out a basic wing for each of them. The Sunrunners do little to confirm or deny any of the rumors of their true size and strength. They have found that the imagination of the general populace does a lot to enhance their already impressive reputation. The air of mystery that surrounds them does as much to help their cause as does their skill in the field.

## Objectives and Policies

### Homeward Bound

Even after the decades of flight and living in the carriers, the Sunrunners still consider themselves the rightful inhabitants of Barat-Tuul. They hold as their ultimate goal, the retaking of their homeworld from the Grubs. To this end, they have created a wide network of associates and developed a range of new tools, including several weapons and ships. Some of these people and tools are designed to maintain

and increase their fighting and survival abilities while living as nomads. Others are targeted at the actual recapture of Barat-Tuul.

The ultimate goal of the Sunrunners is to develop a fighting force of 10 wings, each accompanied by a fully equipped and staffed carrier. At present, they have three full carriers—the *Maelstrom*, *Huntress*, and *Vulcan*—acting as bases for their mercenary forces. A fourth, the *Crescent Moon*, has been converted into an andrite refinery and mobile shipyard. It carries a minimum fighting force which remains with it, and is not for hire. The location of the *Crescent Moon* is kept secret.

In addition to the four carriers, the Sunrunners have managed to acquire several small moons and asteroids scattered throughout the Frontier and even into the fringes of the Backnet. The planetoids have been converted into production facilities, and are principle shipyards for the Coring and newer Kip-Kanzer fighters. There are also two new carriers under construction, as well as, reportedly, enough fighters to supply a force for each. While the factories are most likely able to produce enough ships to pilot the planned 10-wing fleet, their production has been mostly geared towards the production of ships for sale to other governments. In doing this, they have built up a stockpile of funds and materials which will, at a later date, be turned over fully to the growth and armament of the full Sunrunner fleet. The location of these factory worlds remains a secret. So far, no one not of the Sunrunners has ever been to or near one of these worlds and returned with the information.

In addition to their physical tools, the Sunrunners have developed a vast network of intelligence and information gathering. Through this network, they have access to the workings of the great and lesser houses, as well as many of the corporate houses. One of the results of this is that the Sunrunners have what is guessed to be the largest and most accurate database on the Night Brood, its society, tactics, technology, and biology. They are hesitant, however, to share any of their information with others, fearing the release of their data could compromise their information network.

With this knowledge has come the understanding that their former home Barat has become a grub nesting site. They know, therefore, that their chances of reclaiming their home at their current strength are nonexistent.

## Terms of Engagement

The following is a copy of the standard fighting agreement between the Sunrunners and the hiring agency:

*This contract is to formalize the verbal agreement that the hiring agency wishes to employ a Sunrunner force or portion thereof to fight in military battle until the agreed upon objectives are attained, those objectives to be listed below.*

*The Sunrunners will engage in ship-to-ship battle any force desired, with the exception of other Sunrunners or an agency with which the Sunrunners have an active contract. Certain agencies may be exempt from attack from Sunrunner forces due to prior agreements. This contract IN NO WAY exempts the hiring agency from later action from Sunrunner forces.*

*In exchange for the fulfillment of the agreed upon objectives, the hiring agency agrees to pay to the Sunrunners replacement cost for fuel and weapons used in the course of the engagement (this may be paid with actual replacement materials if so desired) PLUS a fee, in cash or trade, equal to ¼ the PURCHASE PRICE of any enemy ships engaged during the period that this contract is in force.*

*IN ADDITION, the Sunrunners claim as reward, the salvage rights to any and all ships, weapons or other equipment belonging to the enemy force. Any such items previously belonging to the hiring agency or any other agency but being used by the enemy at the time of engagement will be considered to be enemy property and subject to the conditions of salvage unless previously agreed upon.*

*In regards to all aspects of the engagement and other times falling within the period of this contract, the Sunrunners remain an INDEPENDENT FIGHTING FORCE, and are IN NO WAY subject to any rules or authority of the hiring agency.*

*All debts, unless otherwise stipulated, are to be paid within one week of the completion of the assigned objectives.*

*If the stipulated objectives are not met, the hiring agency need only pay fuel and weapons replacement. Under such circumstances, the Sunrunners still lay claim to all salvage rights as stated above.*

*Failure to meet and uphold these terms, as stated, on the part of the employer, will be subject to military reprisal by the Sunrunners, in force.*

This simple contract is all the Sunrunners use in the their dealings with the hiring agencies. Early in their existence, the Sunrunners had problems with lawyers attempting to default on their contracts by using legal loopholes. On the first two occasions, the Sunrunners hired lawyers of their own to fight through legal channels. On the third occasion, the Sunrunner representative pulled out his blaster and killed the opposing lawyer. From that point on, this became the official response. Word spread quickly, and there have been very few incidents since.

## Spoils of War

A primary source of replacement ships and parts inventory is the salvage of enemy vessels. To facilitate this, several modifications have been made to the structure of the Sunrunners force. One of these is the installation of a salvage-reclamation facility on each of the carriers. This facility allows the crews to take salvaged ships and equipment, and either repair them to add to the force or "cannibalize" them for parts to repair other ships. The specialized weapons developed and used by the Sunrunners are discussed on page 22.

The salvage brought onto the ships is divided into four categories: ships, weapons, equipment and scrap. The scrap is separated as well as possible, then reprocessed or compacted down and sold at the earliest opportunity. The scrap from a ship can be sold for about 1/10 of its purchase price, though price will vary, and is higher in systems which are mineral poor. In game terms: for each ships which is salvaged as scrap, 1/10 of its BPV can be put towards the purchase of new ships or equipment.

Retrieved ships, weapons, and equipment are repaired if possible. If not, all useful parts are pulled from them and used for repair of other equipment, and the remainder is added to the scrap piles. If a ship is captured without destroying it, any unfired torps and missiles which are considered to be still useable, are transferred to any ship equipped to wield them. In the case of cannon weapons, only those which sustained no damage during the battle can be re-mounted on other ships. The parts of those that were damaged are used for repairs on Sunrunner weapons. Those which were destroyed are turned into scrap. It takes, on average, the parts from three salvaged weapons to repair one damaged one.

## With Your Shield or on It

The Barat disapproved heavily of losing. In fact, they really hate it. They had adopted an attitude similar to that of the ancient Greeks in this respect and believe strongly in the ideal of returning with their shields or on them—victorious or dead. A Barat fighting force would not break off an engagement short of the intended goal unless specifically ordered to do so by their commanders. Even then, they may have disregarded those orders. If defeat is the likely outcome of a battle, the fighters turned to desperation tactics, including ramming. An engaged force often fought to the last ship.

Now, in these leaner times, the Sunrunners have had to adopt a more long-sighted set of tactics. It is now not unheard of for commanders to order a strategic withdrawal from a hopeless battle. Crews that disobey these orders are punished harshly with exile, enslavement, and sometimes venting.

## Prisoners of War

One major rule which the Barat believed in was "take no prisoners". Enemy crews which were taken alive were ejected into space.

Sunrunners deplore waste, and their precarious position has forced them to use every precious resource. It was only logical therefore, that they should come to look upon their prisoners as a lucrative source of income. Ransom can take a variety of forms, from cash, equipment, and services (including favors), and information. (For game purposes ransom is ¼ to ½ the pilot value.) Military information is especially prized, though few captured pilots actually have any information of value. When governments refuse to pay ransoms, captured pilots often turn traitor and try join the Sunrunners, offering information or their skills to their captors.

Ransomed prisoners are released under the condition that they not return to active duty for the period of one month and never bear arms against the Sunrunners again. The ransom for someone who has been recaptured is naturally higher. Occasionally, recaptured prisoners are "vented." (Venting is expelling someone into deep space without a pressure suit.)

Those prisoners who are not ransomed have few alternatives. A few troublemakers are vented. Most, however, become slaves, filling nonessential noncombat roles. In a galaxy devastated by grubs, manpower is in short supply, especially on the fringes of Terran space. Slaves among the Sunrunners work in the fields of terraformed planets, labor in factories, or toil in the mines. Some are sold; rumors abound that the House of Colos is a consistent buyer. Slaves can theoretically earn their freedom, but it takes over a decade.

Only a small number of captives are recruited into the Sunrunners. A member of the Sunrunners must vouch for the prisoner and offer him a place among the mercenaries. Captives who are willing to join the Sunrunners undergo extensive screening and testing. The handful that are deemed worthy and trustworthy then join training wings. Recruits who serve well can retire after five active years or service of become full members of the Sunrunners. Those who are deemed inadequate are vented.

## Recruitment

Like most Terran organizations, the Sunrunners found that competent and skilled pilots were scarce. Captured pilots make up only a small fraction of the Sunrunner forces, and are insufficient to replace Sunrunners captured or killed in battle. Faced with a rapidly increasing attrition rate, Admiral Bach developed an aggressive recruitment policy. The Sunrunners recruit not only military talent, but technological and scientific know how. Currently, just over half of their members are from Barat; and the remainder have been recruited from other sources.

The first new recruits came from planets that had been allied with the Sunrunners before the coming of the Brood, and military contacts enabled them to hire wildcat pilots and crews. As the Grubs spread, the Sunrunners followed, salvaging resources and manpower from isolated outposts and homeless fighter wings. The Sunrunners foraged on the fringes of the swarm, alway avoiding direct confrontations with the Grubs, but always studying their foes and salvaging what they could.

Ingenious tactics and diverse jobs help the Sunrunners keep their ranks full. Several governments in the Beta-cygnet sector hired the Sunrunners to deal with a group of particularly cunning and troublesome pirates. After cornering the pirates, Admiral Bach promptly offered them berths among the Sunrunners. The pirates changed their names and vacated their hideouts, and the Sunrunners announced that they had destroyed the pirates. All that was left was for the Sunrunners to turn over the pirate hideouts to their employers and collect their paychecks.

Taking former pirates into their ranks has paid off handsomely. They used the expertise of their new "colleagues" to set up a network of contacts among other pirate bands. The Sunrunners then used the network to infiltrate at least a half a dozen pirate organizations on which planetary governments had placed high bounties. To date, three of these pirate bands have been absorbed into the ranks of the Sunrunners.

Sometimes, fortune favored the Sunrunners and recruits literally fell into their lap. During an encounter with a fighter wing of the Luches Utopia, the Sunrunners watched in fascination as the entire wing turned on the Luches command ships and utterly the destroyed them. The outnumbered Sunrunners were never even given a chance to engage the enemy. The Luches fighters then surrendered to the mercenaries. When the Sunrunners removed the restraint collar from the captured pilots, they all offered to join the force. Only two troublemakers from the Luches wing had to be vented.

The Sunrunners have on several occasions completely absorbed smaller mercenary forces. These smaller forces are used to fill out wings on their carriers or fill an occasional contract. The Sunrunners have twice outright purchased elements from mercenary wings.

## Strategy

In the realm of strategy, the Sunrunners are renown for their creativity. What seems to be a straight forward attack is often a trap, or an obvious trap is often a bluff. Sunrunner tactics have often caught even their best informed opponents by surprise, due in part to having more Venters & Stingers than normal torps. When in large groups, they like to break into smaller sections and fight on two or more fronts, placing the opponent in a crossfire position if possible. Innovations have been necessary for their survival, after all, what use is a mercenary force that everybody knows how to defeat?

In addition to the ships on active duty, there are any number of additional ships in various stages of repair waiting to fill holes in the ranks. Each carrier tries to maintain a 15% stock of replacement fighters in full functioning order. For purposes of maintaining that replacement stock. A carrier is designed to hold six squadrons plus a flight of specialty ships (a total of 200 ships). At present, each of the three carriers available for hire carries about 128 active ships (four squadrons), the remaining space being assigned to replacement ships and storage of salvage and spare parts.

### Generations

"You want to know what I thought of that? I'll tell you what I thought of that!" A string of obscenities spouted from the mouth of Commander Michael Horst. "If I EVER see that kind of crap again, I'll dry-dock every last one of you dirt-footed punks!"

He walked up to one pilot and stared him down with a look that had become infamous throughout the cadets of the Huntress. "You like that fancy flyin? Is that what you want to do? We're here to kill people, not look pretty. Got that? We don't get bonus points for looking pretty. We get DEAD for looking pretty!"

"You!" Another cade was singled out for his wrath. "Is your brain in your head or in your pants?" The young ma began to shake beneath the commander's burning, stone gaze. "I you had been any close to Vebar's 'jammer you

could have smelled her. I'll give you a hint, boy, if you want to climb all over her, do it when there isn't 200 tons of fighter craft between you!"

His tirade continued for the better part of an hour, each cadet getting a chance to taste the fury of the Commander. The cocky young flyers that had strutted into the hanger in preparation for the day's training exercise, shuffled embarrassed and crestfallen from that same hanger four hours later.

It was a scene that happened over and over in that hanger. Young cadets walked in sure of their ability and their immortality. During the next two years they learned to doubt both of those qualities. At the end, however, the pilots and gunners that walk out of the program do so absolutely sure of their ability—and their mortality. And a new generation of Sunrunners is born.

# New Weapons and Equipment

In the years since the Sunrunners formed, they have developed a small scientific research group dedicated to the development of new weaponry and equipment as well as other technologies which will prove instrumental in the recapturing of their homeworld. The scientific branch of the Sunrunners is housed on several small baseworlds (mostly mined asteroids) and is redundant in its information. No enclave has information that isn't shared with at least one other enclave. In this way, they hope to avoid the drastic loss of information that occurred when Barat-Tuul was destroyed by the Night Brood.

Several of the new weapons developed by the Sunrunners are in a category known as *flash* weapons. These weapons essentially do little physical damage to a ship, but instead knock out its electronic capabilities. Since virtually all aspects of spacecraft are electronically controlled, this has the potential for inflicting large amounts of effective damage while leaving the ship itself in a state to be easily repaired after salvage.

## EMP Cannons

Because of the unique fee charged by the Sunrunners for their services, the salvage, and especially capture, of enemy craft has become important. The first weapon developed specifically to aid in this area was the Electro-Magnetic Pulse Cannon (EMP). EMP weapons were outlawed by the Empire, so they have been added to the Barat arsenal since the loss of Barat-Tuul. The effect of the powerful weapon is to disrupt the electronic systems of the target vessel and disable it while doing little structural damage.

### Game Play

EMP Cannons ignore armor (DR) and do half damage rounded up. Against Brood EMP Weapons do full damage. On a roll of doubles or triples, EMP Weapons do an additional Critical hit.

## Stinger Torpedo

The Stinger Torpedo is similar to the EMP Cannon in that its damage is of a electro-magnetic pulse nature instead of a structural one. Upon detonation, the Stinger releases a large electro-magnetic pulse that cripples the ship's electronics and often kills or seriously impairs the crew. Stingers come in sizes corresponding to standard torpedo marks, Mks.10-50.

### Game Play

Stinger Torpedos ignore armor (DR) and do half high damage round up. Against Brood EMP Weapons do full damage. The number of d12's rolled is the same as a normal torpedo of that MK. For each 12 rolled an additional Critical is done to the target vessel.

## Flak Weapons

A Flak Weapon is any weapon type that targets a location. When it discharges, it leaves a physical hazard on the play area. Flak damage is done during movement phase, just as with asteroids. Flak warheads detonate directly after moving if they have reached their target.

Flak areas may degenerate each turn, eventualy disappearing altogether.

Most Flak Weapons that have any substantial life have physical delivery systems, like torps or missiles.

## Venters

Unlike EMP weapons, Venters are designed to cause purely structural damage to the enemy ship. A Venter is a torpedo with a cache of spent uranium slugs and other scrap metal in place of the traditional warhead. A small explosive discharges the flak in front of the target, forcing the target vessel to fly through it. There are certain advantages and disadvantages to these weapons which make using them a matter of personal preference.

The disadvantages of the Venters are fairly obvious at first glance: they must be fired so as to explode in front of the target vessel, and they aren't entirely successful against better armors. The advantages of Venters are their ease of construction and cheap replacement costs.

Because of their nature, Venters have another special feature: the *Speed Damage Modifier*. This takes into account the drive of the target vessel when figuring the damage, and allows for greater damage to a ship which is traveling at higher speeds.

**Example:** *During the warhead lunch phase Lisa launches a MK30 Venter at the hex in front of Roger's Teal Hawk. During the movement phase, after drive 0 turns but before other ships move, Lisa moves the Venter to the target hex. The Ventor detonates, spreading four Flak tokens. The first counter is placed in the target hex. Then Lisa places a Flack token in the same hex as Roger's Teal Hawk. Roger places one on the far side if the original target hex. Lisa cannot place another Flak token on top of Roger's ship because she has already placed a token in that hex from this torp. She instead places one in the hex to the forward left of his ship.*

## Game Play

Venters are fired during the warhead launch phase like any other torpedo. However they do not target a ship or object, but a location. Designate the target hex with a scrap of paper.

Venters move at the begining of the movment phase, after drive 0 turns, but before ships with drive move. Venters detonate directly after movement.

Venters are "dumb" torpedos designed to be used up close and personal. Because of this they are easy to hit with cannon fire (DV8) and do not ever receive the benefits of hidden torpedo movment.

Campaign note: When resupplying, Venters cost half as much as standard torps.

## Flak Counters

Each Venter gets one Flak Counter, plus one per each 10 MKs of the Torp. The first Flak Counter is placed in the target hex. The player who placed the Venter, and a player on the other side take turns placing Flak Counters. They must be adjacent to one of the Flak Counters in this burst. They may overlap with other Flak Counters that already existed, but they may not overlap any of the flak from this burst.

## Flak Damage

Venters do damage during the ship movement phase, not when they initially explode. Ships entering or turning in a hex with flak, is subject to a 3d6 (High +¼ Drive) attack. To do structural damage, flak must overcome the DV of the target. Each additional flak counter in a hex adds +d6 to hit+1 to damage.

## Dissolution of Flak

At the end of the turn roll a d4 for each Flak Counter. If you roll a 4, it dissolves, and is removed from the board.

## Forward Slow

Ships may move Forward Slow, at one hex per turn, to avoid full flak damage. When a ship is moving Forward Slow the Flak Attack is 3d6 and Damage is Low, +1 per Flak Token. A ship may not move more than one hex during a turn (neither before entering nor after leaving a flack field) and still receive the Forward Slow bonus. Ships that do not move, for whatever reason, receive the Forward Slow modifiers .

**Example:** *In the above example Roger's Tealhawk took no damage when the Flak counter is initially placed in the same hex. If Roger starts his move by moving his Tealhawk one forward or turning, it undergoes a standard Flak Attack (3d6 High +1/4 Drive). If Roger starts his move by sideslipping the Tealhawk to the right it would take no Damage. If he did not move the Tealhawk, or did a forward slow(1 hex), it would take a 3d6 Low attack.*

## The Valkyrie

Among the warriors and technicians of the Sunrunners are a small group of holy women known as the Valkyrie. They live on each carrier and base, set apart from their warrior kin. Theirs is a sacred task; the task of re-claiming the bodies of those fallen in battle and preparing them for their ride to the halls of Valhalla. Once recovered, the bodies of the fallen heroes are cleaned, dressed in their finest battle armor and, after prayers have been said, laid within the funeral pyre. In the millennia since its origin, the ritual has changed only in the details. The warriors ride Wave Cutters instead of stallions, the armor is synthetic composites and the swords changed to blasters, and the blaze of the funeral pyre is now the fiery surface of a star—but it is still a warrior's death.

### Gunboats

Gunboats only take Flak damage to the Damage Track that first entered the hex. If they are stationary within a hex that already has Flak, they take damage to all shields.

# Salvage Claws

The Scorpion is fitted with a pair of Salvage Claws which were originally intended to be used to grasp and manipulate space salvage and other unusual cargo. By use of these versatile tools, the pilot of the ship can safely manipulate space craft or interstellar debris a lot more effectively than could be done with a simple Tractor Beam. Salvage claws can also be used as a weapon, which is one of the reasons that the Renegades retrofitted these ships into the massive war craft that they have become to be known as in the Espan rebellion.

Salvage Claws are attached to the Scorpion by fairly long arms, but they can still only be used as a weapon against another ship at a maximum range of 1 hex. Salvage Claws can be used to attack in two distinctly different ways. Either attack is resolved at the time that the pilot using the claws would attack normally during the cannon fire phase.

## Claw Bash Attack

The first way to attack is to Bash an opponent. This is basically clubbing a ships with the bulky part of the Salvage Claws. The chance to hit a target is 2D6+ADB+1 (you get a +1 because you're using the Scorpion's two claws in concert with each other), and the weapons do Medium+1 damage. The only restriction—besides range, of course, and the fact that the target must be in the Scorpion's front arc—is that the target ship's Drive must be 6 or less.

## Claw Grapple

The second way for Salvage Claws to attack is to Grapple. In this case, the chance for the claws to hit is the same as if they had been used to bash: 2D6+ADB+1. If a hit is scored, the claws do no damage, but they have found purchase on the target ship's hull. The claws cannot be removed until the attacker decides to let go of the target ship or the claws are somehow disabled.

During any movement phases after a successful grapple, the ship with the highest Drive gets to use a number of movement points equal to the difference between the attacker's and the defender's Drive, up to a maximum of 4 points less than the faster ship's current Drive. The other ship does not get to move at all—it has Drive 0 and DV of 5—so the faster ship just gets to drag the slower one as it likes, all over the map. Tight turns cannot be performed while the claws are engaged.

Note that the ship that's not in control cannot perform Drive 0 turns.

**Example:** *An undamaged Scorpion from the Stingers comes up behind a Night Hawk from Death's Symphony which has had its Drive reduced to 5. The Scorpion's player rolls and scores a hit. During the next movement phase, the Scorpion can use up to (11–5=) 6 movement points to move itself and the Night Hawk around however it wants.*

The ship in control can move and turn normally, although it cannot make tight turns. It can even smash the helpless ship into asteroids or ram it into other ships. See Slamming for more on this.

Crews of a Scorpion tend to favor grabbing a victim in a blind spot in its gunnery arcs and then blasting it to pieces with its tail gun. Note that the pilot cannot use another weapon system while the claws are engaged. The claws can be disengaged at the beginning of any movement phase.

The claws can also be used to move friendly ships. If working with a friendly ship, the claws can automatically grab the ship (no need to roll) and then move it up to 4 points less than the Scorpion's current Drive. Alternatively, a damaged Scorpion with little Drive left can hitch a ride on a friendly ship. The ship can then tow the Scorpion around at 4 points less than that ship's current Drive. The Scorpion can let go when it wants to, though.

## Claw Slamming

To slam a ship into another, the Scorpion must first successfully grapple another ship. Then it can ram the other ship into a third ship. This is known as slamming.

Once you've got a ship in your Scorpion's claws, wait for the target of your slam to move. Then move the ship in the claws into a hex facing the target ship and declare a slamming attempt. Which way the ship in the claws is facing has no effect on the attack. Resolve the slamming attack just like a normal ramming attempt. The Scorpion's pilot takes a -3 to the roll due to the unwieldy nature of the attack.

If the slam hits (the Scorpion's roll beats its opponent's), roll 5D12 (All) damage, no matter what the size of the ship used to slam. This is due to the fact that the Scorpion's mass is behind the attack.

Apply the damage to the slammed ship and the ship in the Scorpion's claws. The Scorpion takes no damage, as the shock asborbers in the claws' arms can soak up the impact.

The maximum amount of damage that can be done is the total number of boxes on the smaller ship's damage track. If the captured ship survives the attack, the Scorpion pilot must roll less than his or her Piloting on 1D10 to maintain the claws' grasp on the ship. Otherwise, the captured ship breaks free.

Similarly, if a Scorpion or a captured ship is rammed, the Scorpion's pilot must roll less than his or her Piloting on 1D10 to maintain the hold.

## Slamming into Asteroids

A Scorpion can also slam a captured ship into an asteroid. This is done by moving the captured ship so that it's right next to the asteroid's hex and then declaring the slam. There is no roll in this case. The captured ship automatically takes 5D12 points of damage. This damage is less than if the ship had simply flown into the hex because the Scorpion needs to keep enough distance to ensure it doesn't get caught up in the cataclysm.

## Tractor Beams

Tractor Beams are electromagnetic devices used to capture and tow or reel in other ships. In order to use a Tractor Beam on another ship, the operator must make a lock-on roll based on the pilot's Gunnery skill (just like with a missile launcher). The Tractor Beam cannot be fired at any ship with a current Drive over 10. Ships with a greater mass than the attacking ship cannot be affected by a Tractor Beam unless they are at Drive 0 or a full stop.

Unlike most weapons, the attack comes at the end of the Missile/Torp Launch Phase. During any subsequent movement phase after the beam has locked on, the attacker can tow the defender's ship a number of hexes up to a maximum of 4 less than the attacker's current Drive.

### Breaking Tractor Beam Lock-ons

There are five ways to break a Tractor Beam:

1) If the two ships are ever separated by more than 10 hexes, the Tractor Beam is automatically broken.

2) Any intervening object that would normally block line of site, such as an asteroid, will disrupt the beam.

3) If the target's drive exceeds 10, the beam breaks.

4) Killing the pilot that operates a Tractor Beam breaks the lock.

5) Any hit that destroys or shorts a Tractor Beam will also break the beam.

**Example:** *Raul Filanto's undamaged Scorpion comes about and plays its Tractor Beam upon a wounded Pit Viper with a current Drive of 8. He rolls a lock on and gets it. Raul can use 7 movement points (4 less than maximum) to move or haul his prey in.*

## Tractor Reeling

Alternatively, the ship with the Tractor Beam can reel in the other ship toward itself at a cost of one movement point per hex. Or it can perform a combination of these maneuvers.

The defender's ship cannot move at all—its Drive is 0 and its Defensive Value is 5. No matter what the initiative order may be, the defender's ship moves with the attacker. It doesn't count as a separate and distinct ship for movement order purposes.

As the towing vessel performs its move, the player controlling it has to declare on a hex-by-hex basis how his or her ship is affecting the ship caught in the Tractor Beam. If you wish, you can even allow the distance from your ship to the ship you're towing to increase. Just move away from it and neglect to tow it along with you for any portion of the move that you like. Remember, if the two ships are ever separated by more than ten hexes, the Tractor Beam is automatically broken.

Note also that any intervening object that wound normally block line of sight will also disrupt the beam. An asteroid, for example, would break the contact.

When being towed (i.e., whenever the controlling player moves his or her ship and declares that the distance between the two ships should be maintained), the towed ship moves along right after the towing ship. If there are several paths that the ship could take to accomplish this, the towing ship's pilot gets to choose the towed ship's path. This also applies when the towing ship reels the towed ship in.

If, during the course of a move, the towed ship enters an asteroid hex, resolve the attack against the towed ship as if it had drifted into the asteroid (roll 5D12 damage). Remember, though, that the Tractor Beam's grip will be broken as soon as the attack is over.

Note that a towed vessel cannot end its move in the same hex as another ship. It can, however, be dragged into another ship (see Slamming below). Also, if a towing ship exits the map, the towed ship must follow it off the map at the next opportunity.

If a ship tows another ship off the board, it cannot return to the board. It's assumed to be busy with the ship in the Tractor Beam.

The Tractor Beam's lock holds turn, until it is broken. The only way the beam can be broken is if the Tractor Beam is disrupted, either ship it's attached to is destroyed, or the attacker shuts the beam off voluntarily. Only one ship can be towed by a beam at a time.

Once the beam is engaged, the facing of either ship has no effect on the towing. The attacker can turn and tow the defender away. Any attempts to reestablish contact once broken have to be made just like a normal attack, i.e., within the standard arc of fire.

Although the defender does not have control of its movement while being towed, the ship can perform Drive 0 turns. It can also fire normally, as can the attacking ship. The crew member operating the Tractor Beam cannot operate any other weapons system until the beam's hold is broken or voluntarily disengaged.

## Tractor Slamming

Tractor Beams can be used to slam captured ships into other ships. Just move the captured ship next to a ship that's already moved and declare the slamming attempt.

Roll as if the pilot of the controlling ship was trying to ram the target ship. Subtract -2 for the unwieldy nature of the attack and subtract an additional -1 for each hex the controlling ship is away from the controlled ship.

If the slam succeeds, treat it as if it were a ram, with the amount of damage based upon the controlled ship's class.

If the controlling ship is rammed, this has no effect on the Tractor Beam, unless the attack disables the beam. However, if the controlled ship is rammed, the pilot of the controlling ship must roll less than his or her Piloting on 1D10 to maintain the beam's hold.

### Slamming into Asteroids

Controlled ships can be slammed into asteroids, too. Treat this as if the ship had drifted into an asteroid (roll 5D12 damage). Note that this will break the beam's grip.

# Sunrunner Fighter Units

The total strength of the current Sunrunner force is a nominal 384 active fighters grouped in the following way:

 3 wings
 1 wing per carrier
 12 squadrons,
 4 squadrons per wing
 48 flights
 4 flights per squadron
 192 elements
 4 element per flight
 384 fighters
 2 fighters per element

In addition to the 384 ships listed on active duty, there are any number of additional ships in various stages of repair waiting to fill holes in the ranks. Each carrier tries to maintain a 15% stock of replacement fighters in full functioning order. For purposes of maintaining that replacement stock, see *SALVAGE* on page 19. A carrier is designed to hold six squadrons plus a flight of specialty ships (a total of 200 ships). At present, each of the three carriers available for hire carries only 128 active ships (four squadrons), the remaining space being assigned to replacement ships and storage of salvage and spare parts.

# 1st Fighter Wing: the White Wind

All Sunrunner ships dealt with in this book's scenarios are members of the 1st Sunrunner Fighter Wing. The White Wind is based from the carrier Maelstrom under the command of Captain Tayedor Bach, the son of Tomass.

## Squadron Summary

### SQUADRON 1: JACOB'S THUNDER

Following in the tradition of his father and grandfather, Jacob Bach leads the first squadron of the White Wind. Because of both his ancestry and his skill, Commander Bach has the respect of the crews under his command. Jacob is known for his harsh tactics and wild nature. Under his command, Jacob's Thunder has gained a reputation even among the Sunrunners. One of the reasons for this is the unique composition of his crews; 18 of the 28 ships in his squadron are flown by outsiders recruited into the ranks—fully half of those women. Jacob feels that women make better pilots, having skill equal to or better than men, and without the tendency to take foolish risks. Jacob, himself, tends to take many risks, but he is confident in his own skills and his luck.

**Squadron Leader:**
 Jacob Bach, [Wavecutter]
 (Plt 9, Gnr 6, Lck 10)

**Assets**:
North Flight
   2 x Wavecutter
   1 x Hell Bender
   1 x Night Hawk
   1 x Death Wind
   1 x Spirit Rider
South Flight
   2 x Wavecutter
   1 x Hell Bender
   1 x Night Hawk
   1 x Salamander
   1 x Havok
   1 x Thunderbird
East Flight
   1 x Night Hawk
   1 x Sorenson III
   1 x Hell Bender
   1 x Havok
   1 x Salamander
   2 x Wavecutter

## More Than Just Warriors

When a person thinks of the Sunrunners, they think of warriors; mercenaries fighting for the love of blood and money. There is more to these warriors, though, than the lust for battle and hatred for the Brood. The carriers that have become home to the nomadic mercenaries are full spacefaring communities. Within these communities are most of the activities found in the smallest town and largest city planet-side.

The pub, open 25 hours a day, is the center for social gathering. Over tall stein of ale, the crews sit and talk about the events of the day, brag about their accomplishments in the last battle, and struggle through the ever-complex dance to meet members of the opposite sex.

Sporting teams organized by squadron, crew, or other criteria, including none, battle against each other, or

# Silent Death

against teams from other carriers on occasion. Violent competitions such as wrestling or boxing are, of course, popular. In addition, though, cargo holds are cleared out to become soccer fields; an empty hanger is an excuse for field events such as the hammer throw or even archery. The competitions aren't limited to the realm of the physical either; 3D chess, othello, and more esoteric games are just as hotly contested, and the outcomes as likely to be argued about over a beer the next night as any other.

Acting and music also play a significant role in this odd culture. The Huntress Symphony Orchestra is an exceptional ensemble; playing ancient classics from the likes of Wagner and Holst, as well as more contemporary composers such as Nelsaak and Goers.

West Flight
    4 x Sorenson III
    1 x Salamnder
    2 x Wavecutter
    1 x Thunderbird

### SQUADRON 2: STORMBRINGER

Stormbringer is the heavy artillery division of the White Wind. Specializing in planetary attacks and defense, Stormbringers are straightforward and stubborn in their tactics. They tend to stick to the head-on pummel-and-crush formula of attack. With the ships at their disposal, this is, perhaps, the best option available to them. Commander Kern is a highly competent commander who often is at odds with Commander Bach in terms of policy and strategy, but he defers to his authority without question when pressed. Most Sunrunners feel that Kern will be the one to eventually take command of the White Wind when Tayedor dies, the consensus being that Jacob will have died long before that comes to pass.

**Squadron Leader:**
    Mikhail Kern [Death Wind]
    (Plt 8, Gnr 7, Lck 3)

**Assets:**
North Flight
    1 x Death Wind
    2 x Sentry
    1 x Pharsii II
    1 xGlaive
    1 x Epping
    1 x Spider
South Flight
    1 x Glaive
    3 x Catastrophe
    3 x Pharsii II
    3 x Hell Bender
East Flight
    3 x Catastrophe
    1 x Sentry
    2 x Hell Bender
    2 x Drakar
West Flight
    1 x Drakar
    2 x Hell Bender
    2 x Glaive
    3 x Sentry

### SQUADRON 3: WINDCLAW

Windclaw is the complement force to Kern's Stormbringer. Comprised of the faster, more mobile ships of the wing, Windclaw is the unit primarily sent out to hunt pirates and escort convoys. Radekt's tactics tend to lean towards those of Jacob Bach—with the limited defensive capabilities of his inventory, the strike and dodge is most successful. In the selecting of his crews, Radekt tends to favor piloting over gunning.

**Squadron Leader:**
    Gregor Radekt [Windjammer]
    (Plt 8, Gnr 10, Lck 7)

**Assets:**
North Flight
    3 x Windjammer
    2 x Wavecutter
    2 x Dart
    2 x Salamander
South Flight
    3 x Windjammer
    2 x Wavecutter
    2 x Havok
    2 x Blizzard
East Flight
    1 x Windjammer
    2 xWavecutter
    2 x Salamander
    2 x Thunderbird
    1 x Teal Hawk
West Flight
    2 x Wavecutter
    3 x Blizzard
    3 x Teal Hawk

### Squadron 4: God's Frost

God's Frost is a catch-all. Comprised of a variety of craft, ranging in both size and fire-power, it can handle almost any situation well, yet has no real area of specialty. The other advantage to this is the lack of a standard set of tactics. Commander Mrotek is known as one of the best tacticians among the Sunrunners. Mrotek knows well how to use her available craft to their best advantage, and generally stays back from the center of the battle to better direct her crews. Mrotek's flights are the ones who usually stand guard around the *Maelstrom* while the others hire out, though God's Frost does see a fair amount of outside action as well as the occasional skirmish against pirates or bounty hunters who attack the *Maelstrom*.

**Squadron Leader:**
Katya Mrotek [Talon]
(Plt 9, Gnr 7, Lck 5)

**Assets:**
North Flight
   2 x Talon
   2 x Spider
   1 x Seraph
   1 x Catastrophe
   1 x Havok
   1 x Sentry
South Flight
   1 x Spider
   1 x Havok
   2 x Sorenson III
   3 x Avenger
   1 x Night Hawk
East Flight
   1 x Avenger
   2 x Pharsii II
   2 x Spider
   1 x Havok
   1 x Catastrophe
   1 x Sorenson III
West Flight
   3 x Sorenson III
   1 x Sentry
   2 x Pharsii II
   1 x Havok
   1 x Avenger

# The Next Millenium

It's an impressive sight to see Gustav the Dwarf—a man standing 6'-7" tall and massing over 300 lbs—playing first chair viola. The first chair cellist is a petite, olive skinned young lady of exquisite beauty and skill by the name of Aja Michella—also known as the Little Death; a woman who holds the record for the most registered kills in a single battle.

# Frontier Units

## BETHAN 82ND DEFENSIVE GROUP
### "MANSLAYERS"
**Commanding Officer:** Katriana Kelly

Commander Kelly's Manslayers earned their name after the War when Bethany was still weak from the pounding given them by the Grubs. During that time, a large number of pirate ships chose Bethany as an easy target. After a series of raids which severely damaged Bethany's recovery, Kelly and her all-female crews took the offensive. With a freshly equipped squad of fighters—the last new ships on the planet—the women proceeded to root out the pirates holing up in the system, and destroy them. They let a few of the Pirates to escape in heavily damaged ships in order to let the story spread. Soon after, reports of the "Manslayers" filtered back to Bethany. As a result of their action, the pirate raids diminished radically, and the Bethan were able to struggle back to self-sufficiency unharrassed. Since that time, Commander Kelly has been in charge of the defense of the planet. Even though she holds the actual rank of admiral, she is still referred to as "Commander," and flies most missions with her crew.

## Squadron Summary

Typical pilot (Plt 8, Gnr 5, Lck 4)
Typical gunner (Gnr 7)

### SQUAD 1

**Squadron Leader:**
    Terry Frye  (Plt 10, Gnr 7, Lck 8)
**Assets:**    6 x Salamander
    2 x Spirit Rider
    2 x Revenge

### SQUAD 2

**Squadron Leader**
    Nichole Kinlen (Plt 9, Gnr 7, Lck 10)
**Assets:**    6 x Salamander
    2 x Spirit Rider
    2 x Revenge

## BOKCHI 45TH HEAVY ARTILLERY WING
### "DEMON'S SLEDGE"
**Commanding Officer:** Anna Techau

The Bokchito 45th Heavy Artillery Wing is a force designed for massive destruction of fixed target. Some of the uses of the wing are the temporary defense of important outposts and the interception and repulsion of advancing hostiles. Its primary use, however is to beat down the defenses of a planet or outpost, weakening it for the second wave of surgical strikes and eventual ground forces. The tactics of the 45th are simple: hit hard and fast.

## Squadron Summary

Typical pilot (Plt 6, Gnr 5, Lck 2)
Typical gunner (Gnr 6)

### SQUAD 1

**Squadron Leader:**
    Rikard Sieg  (Plt7 ,Gnr 7, Lck 5)
**Assets:**    1 x Betafortress
    6 x Revenge
    6 x Epping

### SQUAD 2

**Squadron Leader:**
    Willem Swoboda
    (Plt 8, Gnr 6, Lck 1)
**Assets:**    1 x Betafortress
    6 x Revenge
    6 x Epping

### SQUAD 3

**Squadron Leader:**
    Alvin Thym  (Plt 8, Gnr 5, Lck 6)
**Assets:**    1 x Betafortress
    6 x Revenge
    6 x Epping

### SQUAD 4

**Squadron Leader:**
    Brandon Vargas (Plt 7, Gnr 5, Lck 2)
**Assets:**    1 x Betafortress
    6 x Revenge
    6 x Epping

## BOKCHI 29TH PLANETARY ASSAULT WING "IRON RAIN"

**Commanding Officer:** William Noll

This wing is essentially the same as "Demon's Sledge" only more specialized in its use. The only purpose of the Iron Rain is to beat a planet into submission. This wing, and others like it, have been used against enemies and subjects alike several times in Bokchito's history, the planetary assault wings have been used to quell revolts. In the years since the War, they have also been used by the central government to resume and maintain control.

## Squadron Summary

Typical pilot (Plt 6, Gnr 4, Lck 5)
Typical gunner (Gnr 6)

### SQUAD 1

**Squadron Leader:**
Carmen Schill (Plt 8, Gnr 5, Lck 5)

**Assets:**  2 x Betafortress
4 x Sorenson III
2 x Revenge
6 x Seraph

### SQUAD 2

**Squadron Leader:**
Kristopher Schuh
(Plt 7, Gnr 5, Lck 4)

**Assets:**  2 x Betafortress
4 x Sorenson III
2 x Revenge
6 x Seraph

### SQUAD 3

**Squadron Leader:**
Kathryn Schuh
(Plt 6, Gnr 5, Lck 6)

**Assets:**  2 x Betafortress
4 x Sorenson III
2 x Revenge
6 x Seraph

### SQUAD 4

**Squadron Leader:** Thurman Meredith
(Plt 6, Gnr 4, Lck 3)

**Assets:**  2 x Betafortress
4 x Sorenson III
2 x Revenge
6 x Seraph

## PRAGUE 91ST ADVANCE FIGHTER WING "RED TIDE"

**Commanding Officer:**
Vaclav Brezhenevitch

Having been a political satellite of Bokchito for so long, Prague has developed its military systems in much the same way as its former ally. The 91st Advance Fighter Wing is one of the second wave of attack forces sent against a planet under siege. While the Red Tide is an excellent outfit, they have done little to make them stand out from the other wings. The tactics of Commander Brezhenevitch are by the book, and he rarely pushes his men into any situations which would require desperation-type tactics.

## Squadron Summary

Typical pilot (Plt 5, Gnr 6, Lck 7)
Typical gunner (Gnr 7)

### SQUAD 1

**Squadron Leader:**
Adolf Mehorczkk
(Plt 6, Gnr 10, Lck 1)

**Assets:**  4 x Spider
6 x Seraph

### SQUAD 2

**Squadron Leader:**
Merlin Kudek  (Plt 10, Gnr 7, Lck 4)

**Assets:**  4 x Spider
6 x Seraph

### SQUAD 3

**Squadron Leader:**
Mikhail Gosz (Plt 9, Gnr 8, Lck 9)

**Assets:**  4 x Spider
6 x Seraph

### SQUAD 4

**Squadron Leader:**
Peotr Kazik (Plt 8, Gnr 8, Lck 4)

**Assets:**  4 x Spider
6 x Seraph

The Next Millenium

## RATTANNI PEOPLE'S LIBERATION FORCE
### RPLF
**Commanding Officer:**
Jeffrey Kauffman

The Rattanni People's Liberation Force—RPLF—is a revolutionary force funded and supplied by the Bokchi. They hold as their goal the normal demands of such organizations: free and democratic elections, release of all political prisoners, the execution of the current leaders as war criminals, and the abolition of poverty. In reality, they are merely seeking to place themselves in power and reap the benefits of it. Unlike many other revolutionaries, these are well trained—many are deserters from the navy—and well supplied. They have become a major thorn in the side of the Rattanni government. Because of political situations, however, Rattan is unable to send more than a token force against them without severe political repercussions. The RPLF has used this situation to their advantage quite well.

Typical pilot (Plt 4, Gnr 5, Lck 6)
Typical gunner (Gnr 7)

### SQUAD 1
**Squadron Leader:**
James Liska (Plt 6, Gnr 2, Lck 8)
**Assets:** 4 x Talon
6 x Spirit Rider

### SQUAD 2
**Squadron Leader:**
Bao Lor (Plt 7, Gnr 10, Lck 7)
**Assets:** 4 x Talon
6 x Spirit Rider

### SQUAD 3
**Squadron Leader:**
Robin Madsen (Plt 4, Gnr 6, Lck 9)
**Assets:** 4 x Talon
6 x Spirit Rider

### SQUAD 4
**Squadron Leader:**
Kim Neveu (Plt 6, Gnr 3, Lck 6)
**Assets:** 4 x Talon
6 x Spirit Rider

## TABER 23RD DEFENSIVE WING
### "SCREAMING MIMI"
**Commanding Officer:** John Sarosiek

Taber's 23rd Defensive Wing is one of several wings sent out to protect recently acquired territories from being reclaimed by former overlords or taken by other powers while still weak. Their major functions involve openly displaying their presence in order to dissuade attempts at attack. Because this tactic has a tendency to be fairly effective, the defensive wings have little actual battle experience.

Typical pilot (Plt 5, Gnr 5, Lck 4)
Typical gunner (Gnr 6)

### SQUAD 1
**Squadron Leader:**
Dayne Wahl (Plt 5, Gnr 8, Lck 4)
**Assets:** 4 x Sentry
8 x Sorenson III

### SQUAD 2
**Squadron Leader:**
Neil Zuege (Plt 4, Gnr 6, Lck 2)
**Assets:** 4 x Revenge
8 x Lance Electra

### SQUAD 3
**Squadron Leader:**
Michelle Miceli (Plt 6, Gnr 2, Lck 1)
**Assets:** 2 x Drakar
10 x Spirit Rider

### SQUAD 4
**Squadron Leader:**
Kieff England (Plt 8, Gnr 7, Lck 7)
**Assets:** 4 x Pharsii II
8 x Hell Bender

## Weapon Table

| Weapon | Attack Dice | Range Increments (To Hit Modifiers) Short (+1) | Medium (±0) | Long (−1) | Target Speed Restriction | Damage |
|---|---|---|---|---|---|---|
| *Mass Drivers* | | | | | | |
| **Minigun** | 2D6+ADB | 1–2 | 3–5 | 6–12 | — | Low† |
| **Autocannon** | 2D6+ADB | 1–3 | 4–10 | 11–24 | Drive ≤ 10 | Medium† |
| **Railrepeator** | 2D6+ADB | 1–4 | 5–15 | 16–36 | Drive ≤ 6 | High† |
| *Lasers* | | | | | | |
| **Pulse Laser** | 2D8+ADB | 1–3 | 4–9 | 10 | — | Low |
| **Meld Laser** | 2D8+ADB | 1–6 | 7–18 | 19–20 | Drive ≤ 12 | Medium |
| **Turbo Laser** | 2D8+ADB | 1–9 | 10–25 | 26–30 | Drive ≤ 8 | High |
| *Blast Cannons* | | | | | | |
| **Splattergun** | 2D6+ADB | 1–2 | 3–6 | 7–10 | — | Medium |
| **Blatgun** | 2D6+ADB | 1–4 | 5–10 | 11–15 | Drive ≤ 13 | High |
| *Disruptors* | | | | | | |
| **Disruptorgun** | 2D8+ADB | 1 | 2 | 3–6 | — | Medium § |
| **Disintegrator** | 2D8+ADB | 1 | 2–3 | 4–12 | Drive ≤ 11 | High § |
| *Ion Cannons* | | | | | | |
| **Impulsegun** | 2D8+ADB | 1–3 | 4–8 | 9–10 | — | High |
| **Ion Ram** | 2D8+ADB | 1–5 | 6–13 | 14–15 | Drive ≤ 15 | All |
| *Plasma Cannons* | | | | | | |
| **Plazgun** | 2D6+ADB | 1–2 | 3–4 | 5–10 | — | All ¥ |
| **Heavy Plazgun** | 2D6+ADB | 1–4 | 5–8 | 9–15 | Drive ≤ 11 | All¥2 ¥ |
| *Energy Bolter* | | | | | | |
| **Protobolter** | 2D6+ADB | 5–8 | 9–12 | 13–16 | Drive ≤ 14 | 10/8/6 |
| *Melee Weapon* | | | | | | |
| **Salvage Claws** | 2D6+ADB | — | 1 | — | Drive ≤ 6 | Med ‡ |
| *Tractor Beam* | | | | | | |
| **Tractor Beam** | — | 1–2 | 3–8 | 9–10 | Drive ≤ 10 | —‡ |
| *EMP Cannons* | | | | | | |
| **EMP Ray** | 2D8+ADB | 1–2 | 3–4 | 5-8 | — | Med/2¤ |
| **EMP Beam** | 2D8+ADB | 1–3 | 4–6 | 7–15 | Drive ≤14 | High/2 ¤ |

† Whenever two of the attack dice roll doubles, multiply the base damage by 2.

§ If the target's Defensive Value has not been reduced by a critical hit, add 1 to its Defensive Value. Also, completely ignore the target's Damage Reduction when resolving a hit.

¥ If the attack dice roll triples, the weapon mount overloads and is destroyed. The target is not affected.

‡ This weapon can be used to tow a target.

¤ Ignores damage reduction. Whenever doubles or triples are rolled on a hit, target takes a critical in addition to other damage.

## Turn Sequencing

**(1)**
**Warhead Launch Phase**
Roll Missile Lock-ons
Launch Missiles
Launch Torps

**(2)**
**Movement Phase**
Make Drive 0 Turns
Drift
Ventors move & detonate
Roll for initiative
Starcraft movement

**(3)**
**Torpedo Results Phase**
Point Defense or dodging
Resolve torp attacks
Deploy decoys or jam

**(4)**
**Cannon Fire Phase**
Gunners fire
Pilots fire

**(5)**
**Missile Results Phase**
Point defense
Resolve Missile attacks
Asteroid drift
Damage control
Flak Dispersal

## Alternate Range Table

| Weapon Type | Point Blank (+2) | Range Increments (To Hit Modifiers) | | | | |
|---|---|---|---|---|---|---|
| | | Short (+1) | Medium (±0) | Long (−1) | Very Long (−2) | Extreme (−4) |
| *Mass Drivers* | | | | | | |
| **Minigun** | 1 | 2 | 3–5 | 6–10 | 11–12 | — |
| **Autocannon** | 1 | 2–3 | 4–10 | 11–20 | 21–22 | 23–24 |
| **Railrepeator** | 1 | 2–4 | 5–15 | 16–30 | 31–33 | 34–36 |
| *Laser Cannons* | | | | | | |
| **Pulse Laser** | 1–2 | 3 | 4–8 | 9 | 10 | — |
| **Meld Laser** | 1 | 2–6 | 7–15 | 16–17 | 18–19 | 20 |
| **Turbo Laser** | 1 | 2–9 | 10–19 | 20–25 | 26–28 | 29–30 |
| *Blast Cannons* | | | | | | |
| **Splattergun** | 1 | 2 | 3–4 | 5–6 | 7–10 | — |
| **Blatgun** | 1 | 2–4 | 5–7 | 8–10 | 11–13 | 14–15 |
| *Disruptor Cannons* | | | | | | |
| **Disruptorgun** | — | 1 | 2 | 3–4 | 5–6 | — |
| **Disintegrator** | — | 1 | 2–3 | 4–6 | 7–12 | — |
| *Ion Cannons* | | | | | | |
| **Impulsegun** | 1 | 2–3 | 4–6 | 7–8 | 9–10 | — |
| **Ion Ram** | 1 | 2–5 | 6–13 | 14 | 15 | — |
| *Plasma Cannons* | | | | | | |
| **Plazgun** | 1 | 2 | 3–4 | 5–6 | 7–8 | 9–10 |
| **Heavy Plazgun** | 1 | 2–4 | 5–8 | 9–10 | 11–12 | 13–15 |
| *Energy Bolt Projector* | | | | | | |
| **Protobolt** | — | 5–8 | 9–12 | 13–16 | — | — |
| *Melee Weapon* | | | | | | |
| **Salvage Claws** | — | — | 1 | — | — | — |
| *Tractor Beam* | | | | | | |
| **Tractor Beam** | 1 | 2 | 3–8 | 9 | 10 | — |
| *EMP Cannons* | | | | | | |
| **EMP Ray** | 1 | 2 | 3–4 | 5–6 | 7 | 8 |
| **EMP Beam** | 1 | 2–3 | 4–6 | 7–10 | 11–14 | 15 |

## Deflection To Hit Modifiers Table

| Defender Is in this Firing Arc of the Attacker | Attacker Is in this Arc of the Defender | | | | | | |
|---|---|---|---|---|---|---|---|
| | F | FQL | FQR | R | RQL | RQR | Target Has Drive 0 |
| Front | 0 | −2 | −2 | +1 | 0 | 0 | +2 |
| Front Quarter Left | −2 | −1 | +1 | +1 | −1 | +1 | +1 |
| Front Quarter Right | −2 | +1 | −1 | +1 | +1 | −1 | +1 |
| Rear | +1 | 0 | 0 | 0 | −1 | −1 | +2 |
| Rear Quarter Left | 0 | −1 | +1 | 0 | −1 | −1 | +1 |
| Rear Quarter Right | 0 | +1 | −1 | 0 | −1 | −1 | +2 |

# ■ CRITICAL HITS

2 — Pilot killed. Crescent may not perform any further actions.

3 — Gunner B killed. Gunner B's weapons can no longer be fired.

4 — Electronic Warfare disabled. Crescent cannot jam tracking torps. Reduce Defensive Value by 2.

5 — Maneuver Thrusters hit. Crescent may no longer make tight turns.

6 — Shields damaged. Reduce Defensive Value by 2.

9 — Pilot's Pulse Lasers damaged. Pilot's weapons suffer a –1 To Hit penalty until the end of the game.

8 — Evade Thrusters hit. Reduce Defensive Value by 3.

9 — Gunner's Pulse Lasers damaged. Gunner A or B's weapons suffer a –1 To Hit penalty until the end of the game.

10 — Pilot dazed. Crescent cannot move until after the next game turn.

11 — Gunner A killed. Gunner A's weapons can no longer be fired.

12 — Reactor hit. Power generator detonates; vessel is destroyed.

# ■ PULSE LASER SPECS

Short Range: 1–3 hexes (+1 To Hit).
Medium Range: 4–9 hexes.
Long Range: 10 hexes (–1 To Hit).

---

# CRESCENT    I.D. ☐

**Crew**
PILOT
Plt:
Gnr:
*Luck*
GUNNER A
Gnr:
GUNNER B
Gnr:

**Pilot**
4 Pulse Lasers (F)
To Hit: 2D8+ADB+3
Damage: Low +3

Decoys: ○ ○ ○ ○
P-D: 1-4[2]
Dmg Con: 1–5

Mk.10 Torps ○ ○ ○ ○ ○

(FQR)

Damage Reduction 2

(RQR)

(F)

Defensive Value 15

(FQL)    (RQL)

Drive: 16

(A)

Tight Turn Cost ___ +3

**Gunner A**
4 Pulse Lasers
(RQL)[R]
To Hit: 2D8+ADB+3
Damage: Low +3

**Gunner B**
4 Pulse Lasers
(RQR)[R]
To Hit: 2D8+ADB+3
Damage: Low+3

DAMAGE TRACK

| 10 | t | W | ◇2 | t | 16 | 15 | W | t | ◇1 | 13 | W | t |
|----|---|---|-----|---|----|----|---|---|-----|----|---|---|
|    |   |   |     |   | 7  |    | W | 4 |     |    | 1 |   |

BPV: 55

---

# CRESCENT    I.D. ☐

**Crew**
PILOT
Plt:
Gnr:
*Luck*
GUNNER A
Gnr:
GUNNER B
Gnr:

**Pilot**
4 Pulse Lasers (F)
To Hit: 2D8+ADB+3
Damage: Low +3

Decoys: ○ ○ ○ ○
P-D: 1-4[2]
Dmg Con: 1–5

Mk.10 Torps ○ ○ ○ ○ ○

(FQR)

Damage Reduction 2

(RQR)

(F)

Defensive Value 15

(FQL)    (RQL)

Drive: 16

(A)

Tight Turn Cost ___ +3

**Gunner A**
4 Pulse Lasers
(RQL)[R]
To Hit: 2D8+ADB+3
Damage: Low +3

**Gunner B**
4 Pulse Lasers
(RQR)[R]
To Hit: 2D8+ADB+3
Damage: Low: Low+3

DAMAGE TRACK

| 10 | t | W | ◇2 | t | 16 | 15 | W | t | ◇1 | 13 | W | t |
|----|---|---|-----|---|----|----|---|---|-----|----|---|---|
|    |   |   |     |   | 7  |    | W | 4 |     |    | 1 |   |

BPV: 55

---

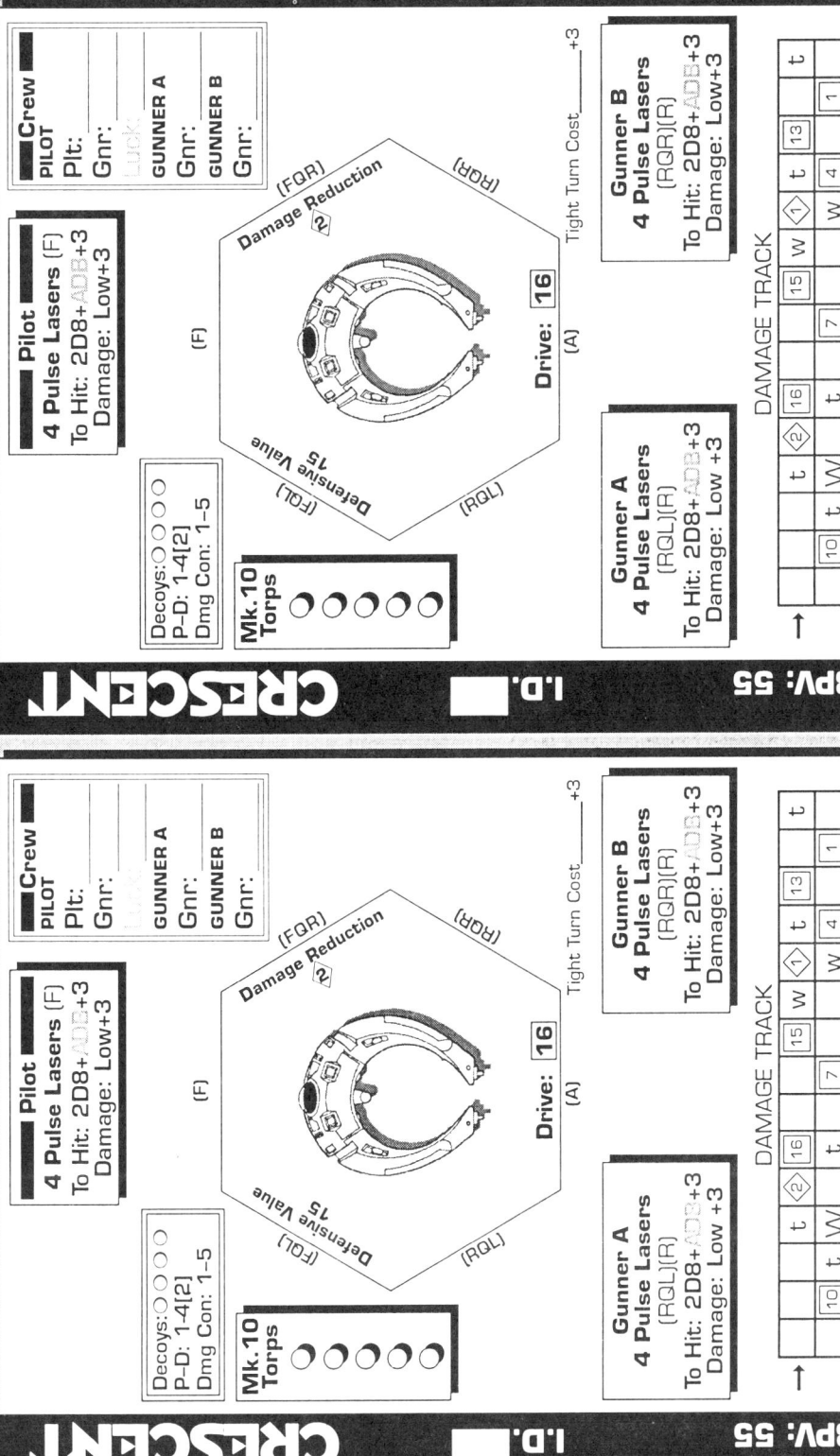

# GAME TURN RECORD TRACK

| 1 | 2 | 3 | 4 | 5 | 6 | 7 | 8 | 9 | 10 | 11 | 12 | 13 | 14 | 15 | 16 | 17 | 18 | 19 | 20 |
|---|---|---|---|---|---|---|---|---|----|----|----|----|----|----|----|----|----|----|----|

Ship Display Updated in *Sunrunners*

## CRITICAL HITS

2 — **Structural collapse.** Curtis Shuttle folds in upon itself and is only a memory.

3 — **Pilot killed.** Curtis Shuttle is able to perform no further actions. Defensive Value drops to 5.

4 — **Electronic Warfare knocked out.** Curtis Shuttle may no longer jam torps. Reduce Defensive Value by 3.

5 — **Maneuver Thrusters hit.** Curtis Shuttle may no longer perform Tight Turns.

6 — **Pilot dazed.** Curtis Shuttle may perform no further actions until after the end of next turn.

7 — **Life Support compromised.** Unless Damage Control is made in the next d4 turns all within this Curtis Shuttle perish.

8 — **Evade Thrusters hit.** Reduce Defensive Value by 4. All turns cost +2.

9 — **Engines destroyed.** Curtis Shuttle may not move or turn. Reduce Defensive Value to 5.

10 — **Defensive Systems down.** All decoys and point defense are lost, and jamming is not possible. Defensive value drops by 2.

11 — **Passenger Compartment implodes.** All passengers are killed.

12 — **Reactor hit.** The universe goes on without the existence of this Curtis Shuttle.

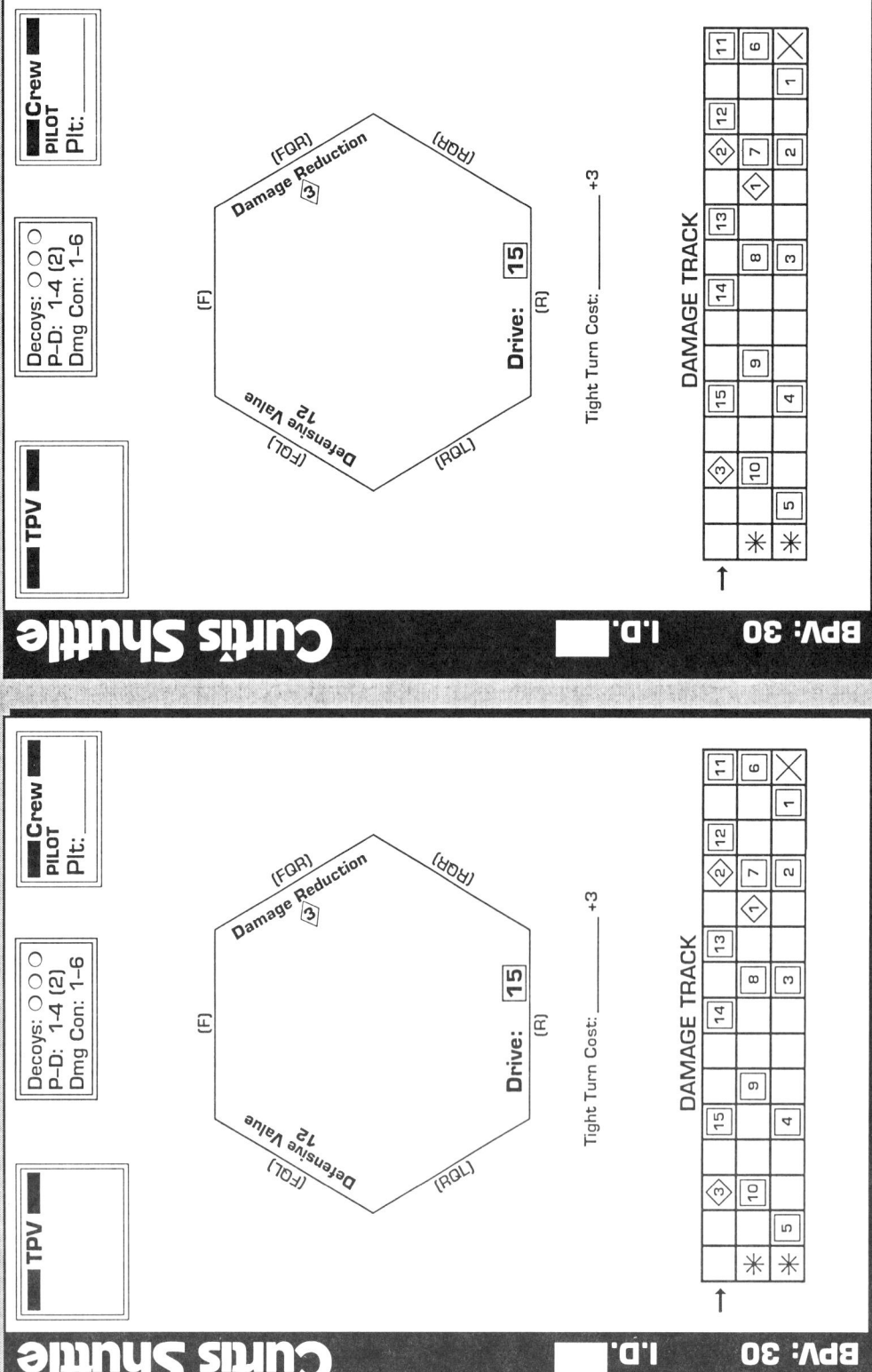

# Curtis Shuttle

**TPV** ____

**Crew**
PILOT
Plt: ____

Decoys: ○ ○ ○
P–D: 1–4 (2)
Dmg Con: 1–6

(FQR)  (RQR)
**Damage Reduction** ③
(F)  (R)
(FQL)  (RQL)
Defensive Value 12

**Drive:** 15

Tight Turn Cost: ____ +3

**I.D.** ☐  **BPV: 30**

**DAMAGE TRACK**

| ③ | 15 | 14 | 13 | ◇2 | 12 | 11 |
| 10 | 9 | | 8 | ◇1 | 7 | 6 |
| ✱ | 4 | | 3 | 2 | 2 | 1 |
| ✱ | 5 | | | | 1 | ✕ |

# Curtis Shuttle

**TPV** ____

**Crew**
PILOT
Plt: ____

Decoys: ○ ○ ○
P–D: 1–4 (2)
Dmg Con: 1–6

(FQR)  (RQR)
**Damage Reduction** ③
(F)  (R)
(FQL)  (RQL)
Defensive Value 12

**Drive:** 15

Tight Turn Cost: ____ +3

**I.D.** ☐  **BPV: 30**

**DAMAGE TRACK**

| ③ | 15 | 14 | 13 | ◇2 | 12 | 11 |
| 10 | 9 | | 8 | ◇1 | 7 | 6 |
| ✱ | 4 | | 3 | 2 | 2 | 1 |
| ✱ | 5 | | | | 1 | ✕ |

## GAME TURN RECORD TRACK

| 1 | 2 | 3 | 4 | 5 | 6 | 7 | 8 | 9 | 10 | 11 | 12 | 13 | 14 | 15 | 16 | 17 | 18 | 19 | 20 |
|---|---|---|---|---|---|---|---|---|----|----|----|----|----|----|----|----|----|----|----|

## CRITICAL HITS

2 — Pilot killed. Windjammer may perform no further actions.

3 — Pilot dazed. Windjammer may not move or fire until after the end of the next game turn.

4 — Electronic Warfare knocked out. Windjammer may no longer jam torps. Reduce Defensive Value by 4.

5 — Maneuver Thrusters hit. Windjammer may no longer make Tight Turns.

6 — Shields damaged. Reduce Defensive Value by 3.

7 — Pulse Laser damaged. Reduce chance To Hit by 1.

8 — Evade Thrusters hit. Reduce Defensive Value by 4.

9 — Engines severely damaged. Windjammer reduced to a Drive value of 1. Reduce Defensive Value by 6.

10 — Engines destroyed. Windjammer may not move or turn. Reduce Defensive Value to 5.

11 — Hull breached. Reduce Defensive Value by 5. At the end of next game turn, Windjammer will disintegrate and be destroyed.

12 — Reactor hit. Power generator detonates; vessel is destroyed.

## PULSE LASER SPECS

Short Range: 1-3 hexes (+1 To Hit).
Medium Range: 4-9 hexes.
Long Range: 10 hexes (-1 To Hit).

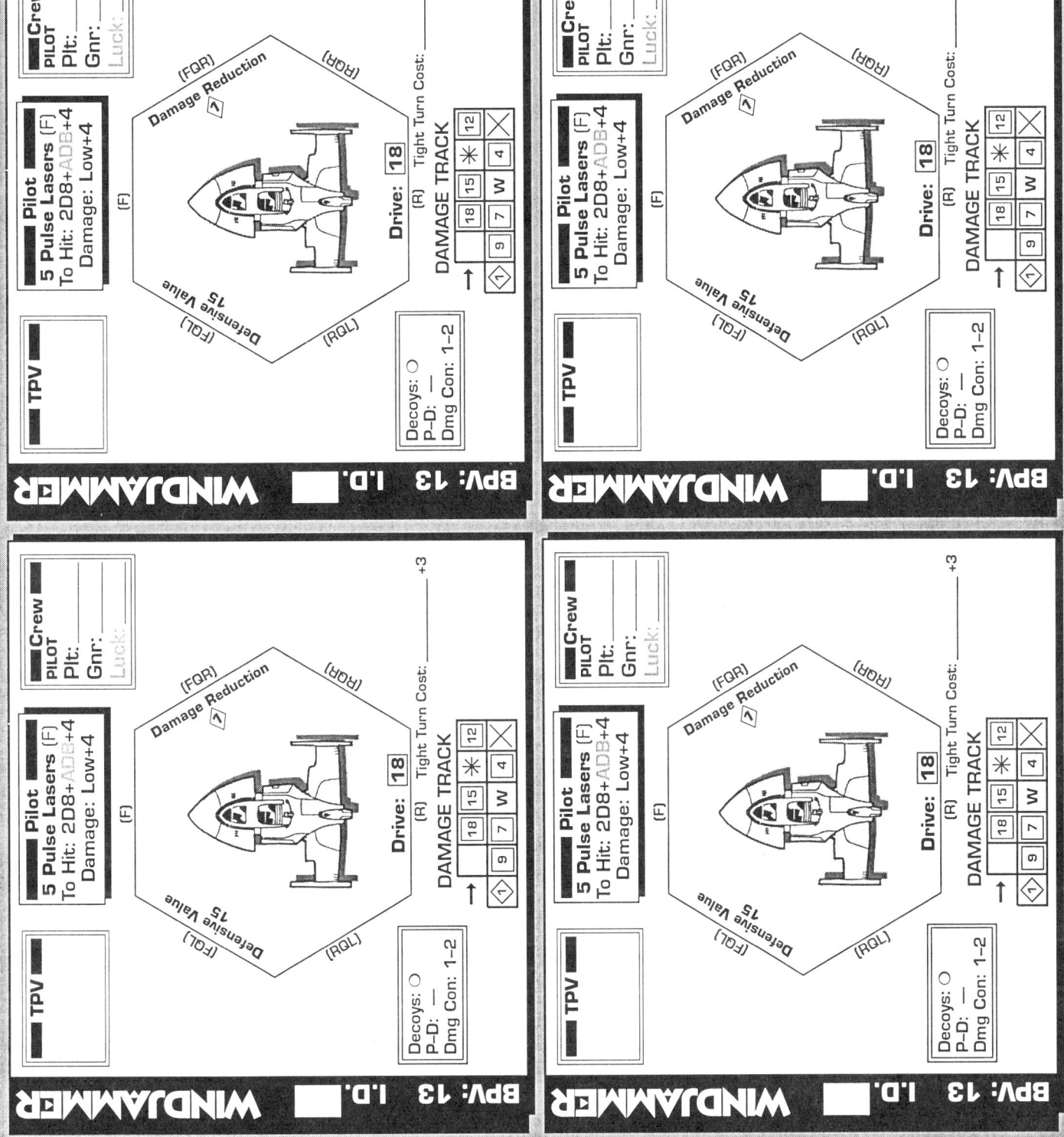

WINDJAMMER   I.D. ☐   BPV: 13

TPV ▬▬

Crew
PILOT
Plt:
Gnr:
Luck:

Pilot
5 Pulse Lasers (F)
To Hit: 2D8+ADB+4
Damage: Low+4

(F)
Damage Reduction  7
(FQR)        (RQR)
Defensive Value 15
(FQL)        (RQL)

Drive: 18   (R) Tight Turn Cost: _____ +3

DAMAGE TRACK

| 18 | 15 | ✳ | 12 |
| 9 | 7 | W | 4 |
| ◇1 | | | ✕ |

Decoys: ○
P-D: —
Dmg Con: 1-2

---

WINDJAMMER   I.D. ☐   BPV: 13

TPV ▬▬

Crew
PILOT
Plt:
Gnr:
Luck:

Pilot
5 Pulse Lasers (F)
To Hit: 2D8+ADB+4
Damage: Low+4

(F)
Damage Reduction  7
(FQR)        (RQR)
Defensive Value 15
(FQL)        (RQL)

Drive: 18   (R) Tight Turn Cost: _____ +3

DAMAGE TRACK

| 18 | 15 | ✳ | 12 |
| 9 | 7 | W | 4 |
| ◇1 | | | ✕ |

Decoys: ○
P-D: —
Dmg Con: 1-2

---

WINDJAMMER   I.D. ☐   BPV: 13

TPV ▬▬

Crew
PILOT
Plt:
Gnr:
Luck:

Pilot
5 Pulse Lasers (F)
To Hit: 2D8+ADB+4
Damage: Low+4

(F)
Damage Reduction  7
(FQR)        (RQR)
Defensive Value 15
(FQL)        (RQL)

Drive: 18   (R) Tight Turn Cost: _____ +3

DAMAGE TRACK

| 18 | 15 | ✳ | 12 |
| 9 | 7 | W | 4 |
| ◇1 | | | ✕ |

Decoys: ○
P-D: —
Dmg Con: 1-2

---

WINDJAMMER   I.D. ☐   BPV: 13

TPV ▬▬

Crew
PILOT
Plt:
Gnr:
Luck:

Pilot
5 Pulse Lasers (F)
To Hit: 2D8+ADB+4
Damage: Low+4

(F)
Damage Reduction  7
(FQR)        (RQR)
Defensive Value 15
(FQL)        (RQL)

Drive: 18   (R) Tight Turn Cost: _____ +3

DAMAGE TRACK

| 18 | 15 | ✳ | 12 |
| 9 | 7 | W | 4 |
| ◇1 | | | ✕ |

Decoys: ○
P-D: —
Dmg Con: 1-2

# CRITICAL HITS

2 — **Structural collapse.** Wavecutter folds up. It is destroyed.

3 — **Engines severely damaged.** Reduce Wavecutter Drive value to (1D4+1).

4 — **Electronic Warfare knocked out.** Wavecutter may no longer jam torps. Reduce Defensive Value by 4.

5 — **Maneuver Thrusters malfunction.** Wavecutter may no longer make Tight Turns.

6 — **Shields damaged.** Reduce Defensive Value by 2.

7 — **EMP Damaged.** If fired Wavecutter takes a critical hit, may fire as normal.

8 — **Evade Thrusters hit.** Reduce Defensive Value by 3.

9 — **Pulse Laser Capacitors overheat.** Wavecutter takes one more hit on damage track due to internal flash fire.

10 — **Controls momentarily lock up.** Wavecutter must move straight ahead at maximum speed next Movement Phase. Afterwards, Wavecutter may move normally.

11 — **Pilot killed.** Wavecutter may perform no further actions. Defensive Value drops to 5.

12 — **Reactor hit.** This ship is gone.

## PULSE LASER SPECS

Short Range: 1–3 hexes (+1 To Hit).
Medium Range: 4–9 hexes.
Long Range: 10 hexes (–1 To Hit).

## EMP Ray SPECS¤

Short Range: 1–2 hexes (+1 To Hit).
Medium Range: 3–4 hexes.
Long Range: 5–8 hexes (–1 To Hit).

¤ Ignores Damage Reduction. Whenever doubles or triples are rolled on a hit, the target takes a critical in addition to other damage.

---

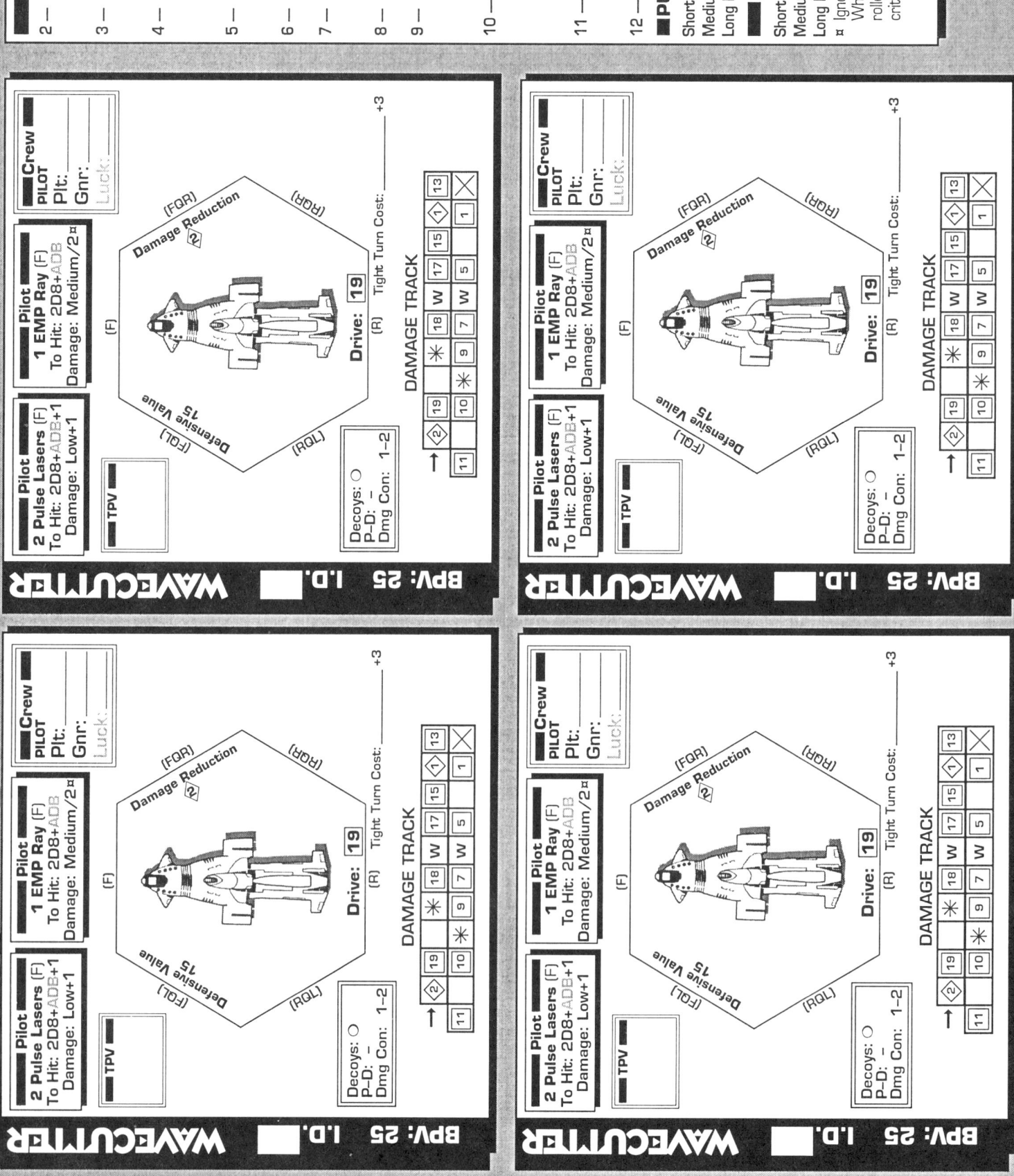

**WAVECUTTER**  BPV: 25  I.D. ☐

**Pilot**
2 **Pulse Lasers** (F)
To Hit: 2D8+ADB+1
Damage: Low+1

**Pilot**
1 **EMP Ray** (F)
To Hit: 2D8+ADB
Damage: Medium/2¤

**Crew**
PILOT
Plt:
Gnr:
Luck:

Damage Reduction ⟨2⟩
(FQR)
(RQR)
(F)
(R)
Defensive Value 15
(FQL)
(RQL)

Drive: 19
Tight Turn Cost: ___ +3

Decoys: ○
P–D: –
Dmg Con: 1–2

TPV

**DAMAGE TRACK**

| | | | | | |
|---|---|---|---|---|---|
| ⟨2⟩ | 19 | 18 | ✳ | 9 | ✳ | 15 | 17 | ⟨1⟩ | 13 |
| 11 | 10 | 7 | W | 5 | 1 | | | | ✕ |

---

**WAVECUTTER**  BPV: 25  I.D. ☐

**Pilot**
1 **EMP Ray** (F)
To Hit: 2D8+ADB
Damage: Medium/2¤

**Pilot**
2 **Pulse Lasers** (F)
To Hit: 2D8+ADB+1
Damage: Low+1

**Crew**
PILOT
Plt:
Gnr:
Luck:

Damage Reduction ⟨2⟩
(FQR)
(RQR)
(F)
(R)
Defensive Value 15
(FQL)
(RQL)

Drive: 19
Tight Turn Cost: ___ +3

Decoys: ○
P–D: –
Dmg Con: 1–2

TPV

**DAMAGE TRACK**

| | | | | | |
|---|---|---|---|---|---|
| ⟨2⟩ | 19 | 18 | ✳ | 9 | ✳ | 15 | 17 | ⟨1⟩ | 13 |
| 11 | 10 | 7 | W | 5 | 1 | | | | ✕ |

---

**WAVECUTTER**  BPV: 25  I.D. ☐

**Pilot**
1 **EMP Ray** (F)
To Hit: 2D8+ADB
Damage: Medium/2¤

**Pilot**
2 **Pulse Lasers** (F)
To Hit: 2D8+ADB+1
Damage: Low+1

**Crew**
PILOT
Plt:
Gnr:
Luck:

Damage Reduction ⟨2⟩
(FQR)
(RQR)
(F)
(R)
Defensive Value 15
(FQL)
(RQL)

Drive: 19
Tight Turn Cost: ___ +3

Decoys: ○
P–D: –
Dmg Con: 1–2

TPV

**DAMAGE TRACK**

| | | | | | |
|---|---|---|---|---|---|
| ⟨2⟩ | 19 | 18 | ✳ | 9 | ✳ | 15 | 17 | ⟨1⟩ | 13 |
| 11 | 10 | 7 | W | 5 | 1 | | | | ✕ |

---

**WAVECUTTER**  BPV: 25  I.D. ☐

**Pilot**
2 **Pulse Lasers** (F)
To Hit: 2D8+ADB+1
Damage: Low+1

**Pilot**
1 **EMP Ray** (F)
To Hit: 2D8+ADB
Damage: Medium/2¤

**Crew**
PILOT
Plt:
Gnr:
Luck:

Damage Reduction ⟨2⟩
(FQR)
(RQR)
(F)
(R)
Defensive Value 15
(FQL)
(RQL)

Drive: 19
Tight Turn Cost: ___ +3

Decoys: ○
P–D: –
Dmg Con: 1–2

TPV

**DAMAGE TRACK**

| | | | | | |
|---|---|---|---|---|---|
| ⟨2⟩ | 19 | 18 | ✳ | 9 | ✳ | 15 | 17 | ⟨1⟩ | 13 |
| 11 | 10 | 7 | W | 5 | 1 | | | | ✕ |

## CRITICAL HITS

2 — **Pilot killed.** Havok may not move, nor may the pilot's weapons fire. Defensive Value drops to 5.

3 — **Engine hit.** Drop Havoks Drive by 5.

4 — **Electronic Warfare gone.** Havok may no longer jam torps. Reduce Defensive Value by 3.

5 — **Maneuver Thrusters damaged.** All turns cost 1 extra point to perform.

6 — **Shields damaged.** Reduce Defensive Value by 2.

7 — **EMP Beam hit.** If fired the Havok also takes a critical hit.

8 — **Meld Laser targeting malfunction.** Modify Meld Laser To Hit attempts by –2.

9 — **Hull buckles.** Reduce Defensive Value by 3.

10 — **Gunner killed.** Gunner weapon skills may not be used.

11 — **Controls lock up.** Havok may not move nor fire until after next game turn.

12 — **Reactor detonates.** Havok is a memory.

### PULSE LASER SPECS

Short Range: 1–3 hexes (+1 To Hit).
Medium Range: 4–9 hexes.
Long Range: 10 hexes (–1 To Hit).

### MELD LASER SPECS

Short Range: 1–6 hexes (+1 To Hit).
Medium Range: 7–18 hexes.
Long Range:19–20 hexes (–1 To Hit).
Target Speed Restriction: Target's Drive value must be ≤12.

### EMP Beam SPECS¤

Short Range: 1–3hexes (+1 To Hit).
Medium Range:4–6 hexes.
Long Range:7–15 hexes (–1 To Hit).

¤ Ignores Damage Reduction. Whenever doubles or triples are rolled on a hit, the target takes a critical in addition to other damage.

Target Speed Restriction: Target's Drive value must be ≤14.

---

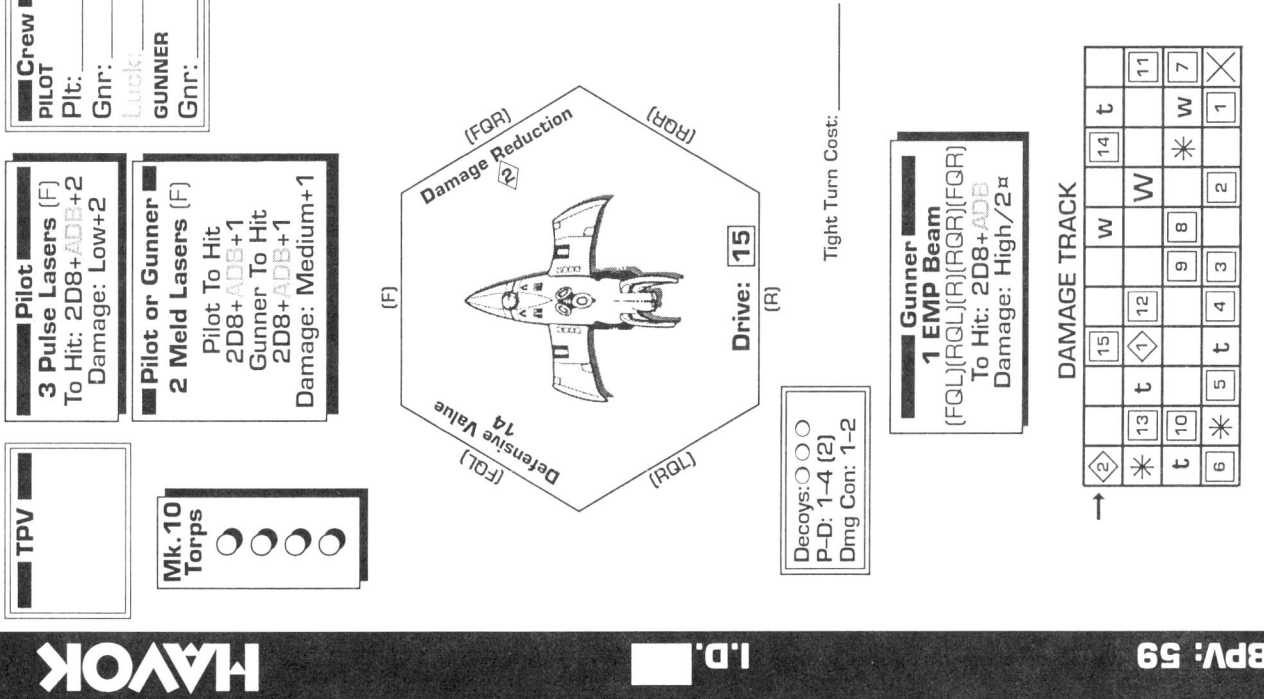

## HAVOK

**I.D.** [ ]

**BPV: 59**

**TPV** [ ]

### Crew
**PILOT**
Plt:
Gnr:  *Lucki*
**GUNNER**
Gnr:

### Pilot
**3 Pulse Lasers** (F)
To Hit: 2D8+ADB+2
Damage: Low+2

### Pilot or Gunner
**2 Meld Lasers** (F)
Pilot To Hit
2D8+ADB+1
Gunner To Hit
2D8+ADB+1
Damage: Medium+1

**Mk.10 Torps** ○ ○ ○ ○

(FQR)          (RQR)

**Damage Reduction** ②

(F)                    (R)

**Defensive Value** 14

(FQL)          (RQL)

**Drive:** 15

Decoys: ○ ○ ○
P-D: 1–4 (2)
Dmg Con: 1–2

Tight Turn Cost: _____ +3

### Gunner
**1 EMP Beam**
(FQL)(RQL)(R)(RQR)(FQR)
To Hit: 2D8+ADB
Damage: High/2¤

### DAMAGE TRACK

| ◇② | ✳ | t | 13 | 10 | ✳ | t | 15 | ◇① | t | 12 | ✳ | 14 | t | 11 |
|---|---|---|---|---|---|---|---|---|---|---|---|---|---|---|
| 6 | t | 5 | 4 | 3 | 9 | 8 | W | w | 2 | 1 | ✳ | W | w | 7 |
| | | | | | | | | | | | | | | ✕ |

↑

---

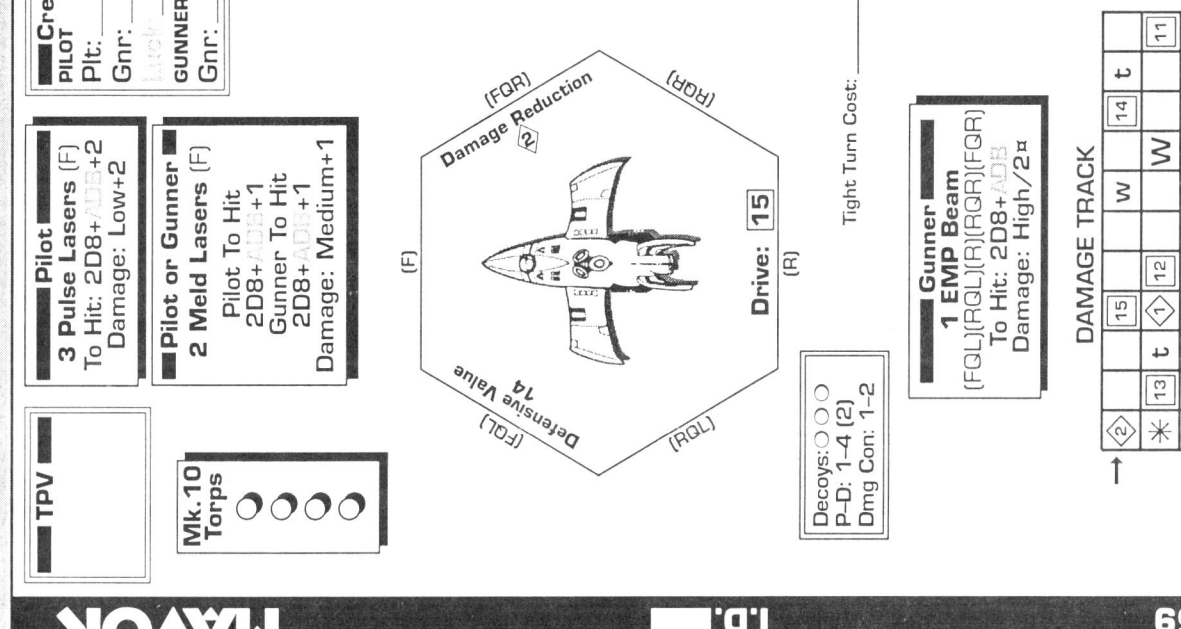

## HAVOK

**I.D.** [ ]

**BPV: 59**

**TPV** [ ]

### Crew
**PILOT**
Plt:
Gnr:  *Lucki*
**GUNNER**
Gnr:

### Pilot
**3 Pulse Lasers** (F)
To Hit: 2D8+ADB+2
Damage: Low+2

### Pilot or Gunner
**2 Meld Lasers** (F)
Pilot To Hit
2D8+ADB+1
Gunner To Hit
2D8+ADB+1
Damage: Medium+1

**Mk.10 Torps** ○ ○ ○ ○

(FQR)          (RQR)

**Damage Reduction** ②

(F)                    (R)

**Defensive Value** 14

(FQL)          (RQL)

**Drive:** 15

Decoys: ○ ○ ○
P-D: 1–4 (2)
Dmg Con: 1–2

Tight Turn Cost: _____ +3

### Gunner
**1 EMP Beam**
(FQL)(RQL)(R)(RQR)(FQR)
To Hit: 2D8+ADB
Damage: High/2¤

### DAMAGE TRACK

| ◇② | ✳ | t | 13 | 10 | ✳ | t | 15 | ◇① | t | 12 | ✳ | 14 | t | 11 |
|---|---|---|---|---|---|---|---|---|---|---|---|---|---|---|---|
| 6 | t | 5 | 4 | 3 | 9 | 8 | W | w | 2 | 1 | ✳ | W | w | 7 |
| | | | | | | | | | | | | | | ✕ |

↑

## CRITICAL HITS

2 — **Crew killed.** Vessel may perform no further actions.

3 — **Engines hit.** Reduce Avenger's Drive by 5.

4 — **Electronic Warfare knocked out.** Avenger may no longer jam torps. Reduce Defensive Value by 2.

5 — **Maneuver Thrusters damaged.** All turns, cost one extra movement point to perform.

6 — **Shields damaged.** Reduce Defensive Value by 1.

7 — **Meld Lasers damaged.** Reduce chance To Hit by 2.

8 — **Torp Targeting offline.** No torpedoes may be fired until after the next game turn.

9 — **Hull breached.** Reduce Defensive Value by 3 and lose two torps of the pilot's choice.

10 — **Gunner killed.** Gunner weapon may no longer be fired.

11 — **Pilot dazed.** Avenger may not move or fire the Meld Lasers until after the next game turn. The gunner may still fire while the pilot is dazed.

12 — **Reactor hit.** Avenger bursts into fiery cloud and is gone.

### MELD LASER SPECS

Short Range: 1–6 hexes (+1 To Hit).
Medium Range: 7–18 hexes.
Long Range: 19–20 hexes (–1 To Hit).
Target Speed Restriction: Target's Drive value must be ≤12.

### EMP Beam SPECS¤

Short Range: 1–3 hexes (+1 To Hit).
Medium Range: 4–6 hexes.
Long Range: 7–15 hexes (–1 To Hit).
¤ Ignores Damage Reduction
Whenever doubles or triples are rolled on a hit, the target takes a critical in addition to other damage.
Target Speed Restriction: Target's Drive value must be ≤14.

---

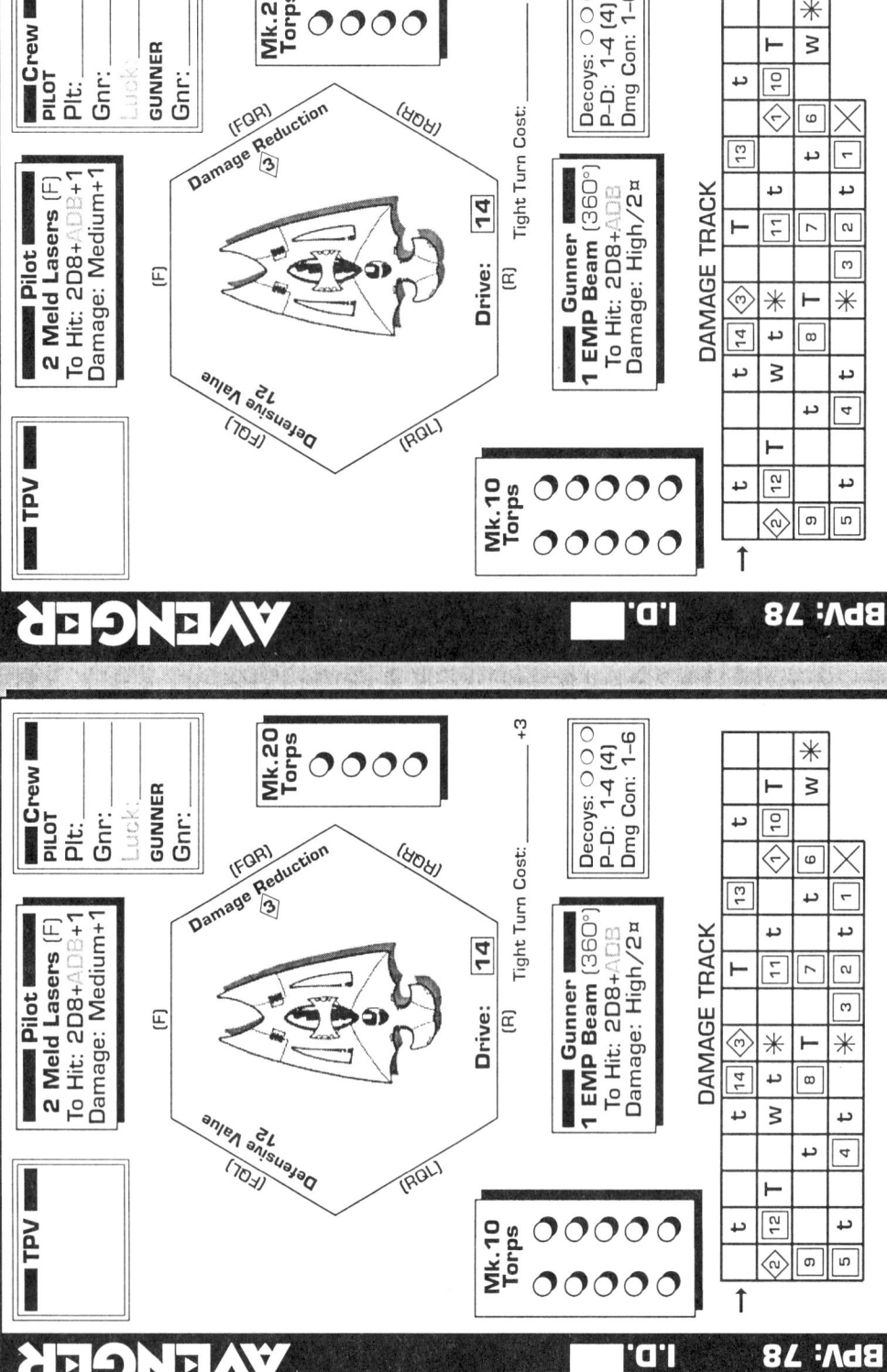

## AVENGER

**TPV** ___

**Crew**
PILOT
Plt: ___
Gnr: ___
Luck: ___
GUNNER
Gnr: ___

**Pilot**
2 Meld Lasers (F)
To Hit: 2D8+AD8+1
Damage: Medium+1

**Gunner** (360°)
1 EMP Beam
To Hit: 2D8+AD8
Damage: High/2¤

Damage Reduction ③

Defensive Value 12

(FQR) (RQR) (F) (R) (FQL) (RQL)

Drive: 14

Tight Turn Cost: ___ +3

Decoys: ○○○
P-D: 1-4 (4)
Dmg Con: 1-6

Mk.20 Torps ○○○○

Mk.10 Torps ○○○○○ / ○○○○○

**DAMAGE TRACK**

**BPV: 78**

**I.D.** ___

---

## AVENGER

**TPV** ___

**Crew**
PILOT
Plt: ___
Gnr: ___
Luck: ___
GUNNER
Gnr: ___

**Pilot**
2 Meld Lasers (F)
To Hit: 2D8+AD8+1
Damage: Medium+1

**Gunner** (360°)
1 EMP Beam
To Hit: 2D8+AD8
Damage: High/2¤

Damage Reduction ③

Defensive Value 12

(FQR) (RQR) (F) (R) (FQL) (RQL)

Drive: 14

Tight Turn Cost: ___ +3

Decoys: ○○○
P-D: 1-4 (4)
Dmg Con: 1-6

Mk.20 Torps ○○○○

Mk.10 Torps ○○○○○ / ○○○○○

**DAMAGE TRACK**

**BPV: 78**

**I.D.** ___

---

## GAME TURN RECORD TRACK

| 1 | 2 | 3 | 4 | 5 | 6 | 7 | 8 | 9 | 10 | 11 | 12 | 13 | 14 | 15 | 16 | 17 | 18 | 19 | 20 |
|---|---|---|---|---|---|---|---|---|----|----|----|----|----|----|----|----|----|----|----|

# SPIDER

I.D. ▮

BPV: 129

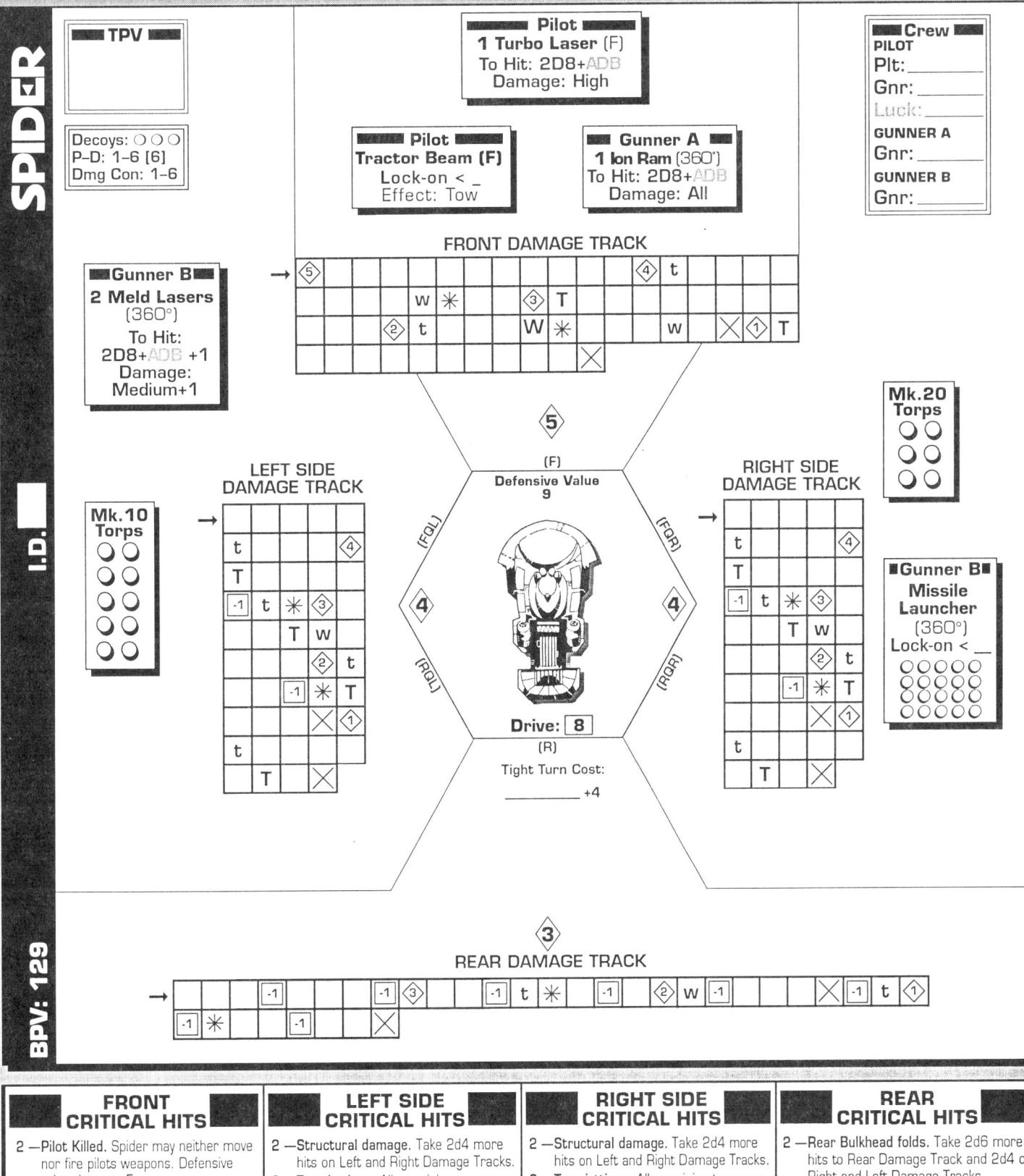

**TPV**

Decoys: ○ ○ ○
P–D: 1–6 [6]
Dmg Con: 1–6

**Pilot**
1 Turbo Laser (F)
To Hit: 2D8+ADB
Damage: High

**Pilot**
Tractor Beam (F)
Lock-on < _
Effect: Tow

**Gunner A**
1 Ion Ram (360°)
To Hit: 2D8+ADB
Damage: All

**Crew**
PILOT
Plt:_____
Gnr:_____
Luck:_____
GUNNER A
Gnr:_____
GUNNER B
Gnr:_____

**Gunner B**
2 Meld Lasers
(360°)
To Hit:
2D8+ADB +1
Damage:
Medium+1

FRONT DAMAGE TRACK

**Mk.20 Torps**
○ ○ ○
○ ○ ○
○ ○ ○

**Mk.10 Torps**
○ ○
○ ○
○ ○
○ ○
○ ○

LEFT SIDE
DAMAGE TRACK

RIGHT SIDE
DAMAGE TRACK

**Gunner B**
Missile Launcher
(360°)
Lock-on < __
○ ○ ○ ○ ○
○ ○ ○ ○ ○
○ ○ ○ ○ ○

(F)
Defensive Value
9

⬖5

⬖4 (FQL) (FQR) 4⬖

(RQL) (RQR)

Drive: [8]
(R)

Tight Turn Cost:
_____ +4

⟨3⟩
REAR DAMAGE TRACK

---

## FRONT CRITICAL HITS

2 —Pilot Killed. Spider may neither move nor fire pilots weapons. Defensive value drops to 5.

3 —Too tough! No extra damage.

4 —Shields damaged. Reduce Defensive Value by 1.

5 —Piloting Controls lock up. Spider may not turn until after next Movement Phase.

6 —Gunner A killed. Gunner A's Ion Ram may not be used.

7 —Cascading Hull collapse. Take 1d6 damage on all Damage Tracks.

8 —Pilot dazed. Spider may not move until after next game turn.

## LEFT SIDE CRITICAL HITS

2 —Structural damage. Take 2d4 more hits on Left and Right Damage Tracks.

3 —Torp jettison. All remaining torps are lost.

4 —Targeting System damaged. All weapons systems suffer -1 To Hit.

5 —Gunner B stunned. Gunner B's weapons may not fire until after next game turn.

6 —Maneuver Thrusters hit. All turns cost 1 extra movement point to perform.

7 —Gunner B killed. Weapons may not fire.

8 —Electronic Warfare gone. Spider cannot jam torps. Reduce Defensive Value by 2

## RIGHT SIDE CRITICAL HITS

2 —Structural damage. Take 2d4 more hits on Left and Right Damage Tracks.

3 —Torp jettison. All remaining torps are lost.

4 —Targeting System damaged. All weapons systems suffer -1 To Hit.

5 —Gunner B stunned. Weapons may not fire until after next game turn.

6 —Maneuver Thrusters hit. All turns cost 1 extra movement point to perform.

7 —Gunner B killed. Gunner B's weapons may not fire.

8 —Electronic Warfare gone. Spider cannot jam torps. Reduce Defensive Value by 2

## REAR CRITICAL HITS

2 —Rear Bulkhead folds. Take 2d6 more hits to Rear Damage Track and 2d4 on Right and Left Damage Tracks.

3 —Maneuver Thrusters hit. All turns cost 1 extra movement point to perform.

4 —Engine Hit. Drive is reduced by half, round up.

5 —Electronic Warfare damaged. Reduce Defensive Value by 2.

6 —Engine destroyed. Drive is reduced to 0 and Defensive Value drops to 5.

7 —Engine Stalls. For next turn only Drive is reduced to 0 and Defensive Value drops to 5.

8 —Reactor detonates. The Spider is consumed in a flash of destruction.

# CATASTROPHE

I.D.

BPV: 142

**TPV**

Mk.10 Torps
Mk.20 Torps

Decoys: ○ ○ ○ ○
P–D: 1–6 [4]
Dmg Con: 1–6

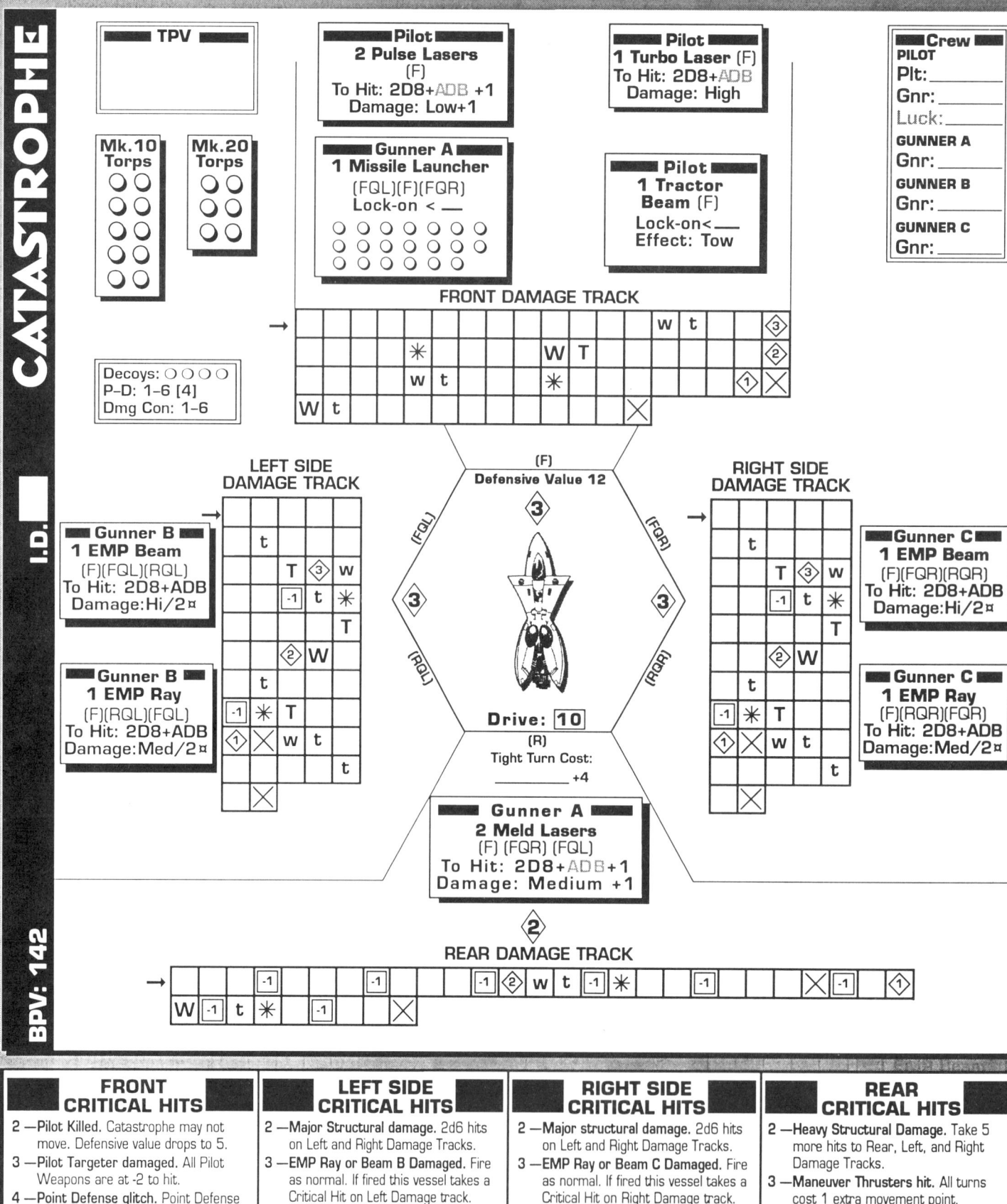

**Pilot**
**2 Pulse Lasers**
(F)
To Hit: 2D8+ADB +1
Damage: Low+1

**Gunner A**
**1 Missile Launcher**
(FQL)(F)(FQR)
Lock-on < ___

**Pilot**
**1 Turbo Laser** (F)
To Hit: 2D8+ADB
Damage: High

**Pilot**
**1 Tractor Beam** (F)
Lock-on< ___
Effect: Tow

**Crew**
PILOT
Plt: _____
Gnr: _____
Luck: _____
GUNNER A
Gnr: _____
GUNNER B
Gnr: _____
GUNNER C
Gnr: _____

## FRONT DAMAGE TRACK

## LEFT SIDE DAMAGE TRACK

**Gunner B**
**1 EMP Beam**
(F)(FQL)(RQL)
To Hit: 2D8+ADB
Damage:Hi/2¤

**Gunner B**
**1 EMP Ray**
(F)(RQL)(FQL)
To Hit: 2D8+ADB
Damage:Med/2¤

(F)
Defensive Value 12
(FQL)  (FQR)
③  ③  ③
(RQL)  (RQR)

Drive: 10
(R)
Tight Turn Cost:
_____ +4

## RIGHT SIDE DAMAGE TRACK

**Gunner C**
**1 EMP Beam**
(F)(FQR)(RQR)
To Hit: 2D8+ADB
Damage:Hi/2¤

**Gunner C**
**1 EMP Ray**
(F)(RQR)(FQR)
To Hit: 2D8+ADB
Damage:Med/2¤

**Gunner A**
**2 Meld Lasers**
(F) (FQR) (FQL)
To Hit: 2D8+ADB+1
Damage: Medium +1

## REAR DAMAGE TRACK

## FRONT CRITICAL HITS
2 —Pilot Killed. Catastrophe may not move. Defensive value drops to 5.
3 —Pilot Targeter damaged. All Pilot Weapons are at -2 to hit.
4 —Point Defense glitch. Point Defense spread drops to 1-5[-1].
5 —Front Armor peels off. Front Damage Reduction drops to 0.
6 —Gunner A Killed
7 —Shields damaged. Reduce Defensive Value by 1.
8 —Pilot dazed. Catastrophe may not move until after next game turn.

## LEFT SIDE CRITICAL HITS
2 —Major Structural damage. 2d6 hits on Left and Right Damage Tracks.
3 —EMP Ray or Beam B Damaged. Fire as normal. If fired this vessel takes a Critical Hit on Left Damage track.
4 —Maneuver Thrusters Stripped. Catastrophe may no longer perform tight turns. -1 Defensive Value.
5 —Torp Load jettison. Loose all remaining torps.
6 —Gunner B Killed.
7 —Left Armor peels off. Left Damage Reduction drops to 0.
8 —Electronic Warfare gone. Catastrophe cannot jam torps. Reduce Defensive Value by 2

## RIGHT SIDE CRITICAL HITS
2 —Major structural damage. 2d6 hits on Left and Right Damage Tracks.
3 —EMP Ray or Beam C Damaged. Fire as normal. If fired this vessel takes a Critical Hit on Right Damage track.
4 —Maneuver Thrusters Stripped. Catastrophe may no longer perform tight turns. -1 Defensive Value.
5 —Torp Load jettison. Loose all remaining torps.
6 —Gunner C Killed.
7 —Right Armor peels off. Right Damage Reduction drops to 0.
8 —Electronic Warfare gone. Catastrophe cannot jam torps. Reduce Defensive Value by 2

## REAR CRITICAL HITS
2 —Heavy Structural Damage. Take 5 more hits to Rear, Left, and Right Damage Tracks.
3 —Maneuver Thrusters hit. All turns cost 1 extra movement point.
4 —Engine Stalls. Next turn only, reduce Drive to 0, drop Def. Value to 5.
5 —Random EMP cannon damaged. Fire as normal. If fired, this vessel takes a Critical Hit on Rear Damage track.
6 —Engine destroyed. Reduce Drive to 0. Drop Def. Value to 5. Engine gone.
7 —Rear Bulkhead folds. Take 4 more hits to Rear Damage Track.
8 —Reactor detonates. With a brilliant flash the Catastrophe is over.

# BORAX FREIGHTER

I.D. ☐

BPV: 18

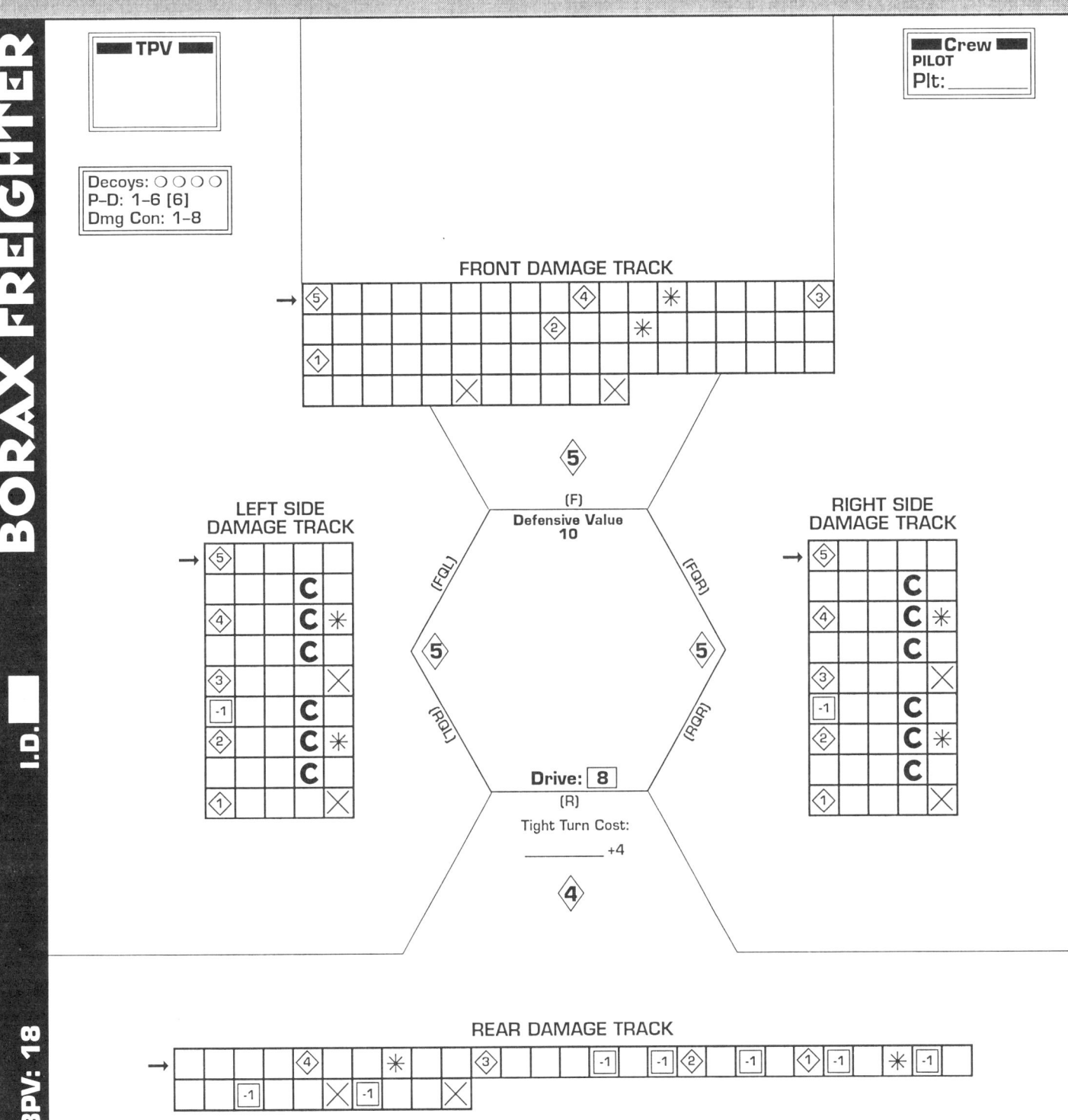

TPV ☐

Decoys: ○ ○ ○ ○
P–D: 1–6 [6]
Dmg Con: 1–8

**Crew**
PILOT
Plt: _____

FRONT DAMAGE TRACK

LEFT SIDE DAMAGE TRACK

RIGHT SIDE DAMAGE TRACK

(F)
Defensive Value
10

Drive: 8
(R)
Tight Turn Cost:
_____ +4

REAR DAMAGE TRACK

## FRONT CRITICAL HITS

2 —**Pilot Killed.** Borax may not move. Defensive value drops to 5.

3 —**Too tough!** No extra damage.

4 —**Decoy short.** All decoys are destroyed

5 —**Too tough!** No extra damage.

6 —**Controls lock up.** Borax must move its full movement in a straight line next turn.

7 —**Life Support compromised.** Unless Damage control is made in the next two turns the crew of the Borax dies.

8 —**Pilot dazed.** Borax may not move until after next game turn.

## LEFT SIDE CRITICAL HITS

2 —**Major structural damage.** Take 2d4 more hits on Left and Right Damage Tracks.

3 —**Cargo Bay chain explosion.** Mark off all remaining C's on Left and Right Damage Tracks.

4 —**Too tough!** No extra damage.

5 —**Too tough!** No extra damage.

6 —**Cargo Bay A implodes.** Mark off all C's on Left Damage Track.

7 —**Defenses crippled.** Borax may not use Point Defense against torps impacting on the Left Damage Track.

8 —**Electronic Warfare gone.** Borax cannot jam torps. Reduce Defensive Value by 2

## RIGHT SIDE CRITICAL HITS

2 —**Major structural damage.** Take 2d4 more hits on Left and Right Damage Tracks.

3 —**Cargo Bay chain explosion.** Mark off all remaining C's on Left and Right Damage Tracks.

4 —**Too tough!** No extra damage.

5 —**Too tough!** No extra damage.

6 —**Cargo Bay B implodes.** Mark off all C's on Right Damage Track.

7 —**Defenses crippled.** Borax may not use Point Defense against torps impacting on the Right Damage Track.

8 —**Electronic Warfare gone.** Borax cannot jam torps. Reduce Defensive Value by 2

## REAR CRITICAL HITS

2 —**Rear Bulkhead folds.** Take 2d4 more hits to Rear Damage Track.

3 —**Maneuver Thrusters hit.** All turns cost 1 extra movement point.

4 —**Engine Chokes.** For next turn only Drive is reduced to 0 and Defensive Value drops to 5

5 —**Too tough!** No extra damage.

6 —**Engine destroyed.** Drive is reduced to 0 and Defensive Value drops to 5 as the engine frees itself.

7 —**Hyper-Drive collapse.** Borax may not engage Hyper-Drive.

8 —**Reactor detonates.** With a silent flash the Borax Freighter and its cargo become radioactive slag.

# EPPING

**I.D.** ▮

**BPV: 119**

**TPV**

Decoys: ○ ○ ○ ○
P–D: 1–7 [3]
Dmg Con: 1–7

## ■ Pilot ■
**1 Meld Laser** (F)
To Hit: 2D8+ADB
Damage: Medium

## ■ Gunner A ■
**4 Pulse Lasers** (F)
To Hit: 2D8+ADB+3
Damage: Low+3

## ■ Gunner A ■
**Missile Launcher**
(360˚)
Lock-on < __
○ ○ ○ ○ ○ ○
○ ○ ○ ○ ○ ○
○ ○ ○ ○ ○ ○
○ ○ ○ ○ ○ ○

**Mk. 30 Torps**
○
○
○
○

## ■ Crew ■
PILOT
Plt:_____
Gnr:_____
Luck:_____
**GUNNER A**
Gnr:_____
**GUNNER B**
Gnr:_____
**GUNNER C**
Gnr:_____

## ■ Gunner B ■
**4 Pulse Lasers**
(FQL)(RQL)(R)
To Hit: 2D8+ADB+3
Damage: Low+3

## ■ Gunner C ■
**4 Pulse Lasers**
(FQR)(RQR)(R)
To Hit: 2D8+ADB+3
Damage: Low+3

### FRONT DAMAGE TRACK

### LEFT SIDE DAMAGE TRACK

### RIGHT SIDE DAMAGE TRACK

## ■ Gunner B ■
**Missile Launcher**
(360˚)
Lock-on < __
○ ○ ○ ○ ○ ○
○ ○ ○ ○ ○ ○
○ ○ ○ ○ ○ ○
○ ○ ○ ○ ○ ○

## ■ Gunner C ■
**Missile Launcher**
(360˚)
Lock-on < __
○ ○ ○ ○ ○ ○
○ ○ ○ ○ ○ ○
○ ○ ○ ○ ○ ○
○ ○ ○ ○ ○ ○

◇4◇
(F)
Defensive Value 12

(FQL) (FQR)
3 3
(RQL) (RQR)

**Drive: 11**
(R)
Tight Turn Cost:
_____ +4

◇2◇

### REAR DAMAGE TRACK

---

## FRONT CRITICAL HITS
2 — **Pilot killed.** Epping may not move nor fire Meld Laser.
3 — **Missile Launcher A malfunctions.** Lose 1D10 missiles.
4 — **Shields damaged.** Reduce Defensive Value by 1.
5 — **Pulse Lasers damaged.** Reduce chance To Hit by 1.
6 — **Meld Laser Targeters damaged.** Weapon may not fire until after next game turn.
7 — **Gunner A killed.** Lose use of Gunner A's weapons.
8 — **Fatal Chain Reaction Explosion.** Blast guts this vessel from the front to the back. Epping is destroyed.

## LEFT SIDE CRITICAL HITS
2 — **Engine sputters.** Epping only has Drive 2 next turn.
3 — **Missile Launcher B malfunctions.** Lose 1D10 missiles.
4 — **Shields damaged.** Reduce Defensive Value by 1.
5 — **Pulse Laser B damaged.** Reduce chance to hit by 1.
6 — **Missile Launcher B damaged.** Weapon may not fire until after next game turn.
7 — **Gunner B killed.** Lose use of Gunner B's weapons.
8 — **Structural Damage.** Take 10 more hits on this Damage Track and 8 more on the Right Side Damage Track.

## RIGHT SIDE CRITICAL HITS
2 — **Engine sputters.** Epping only has Drive 2 next turn.
3 — **Missile Launcher C malfunctions.** Lose 1D10 missiles.
4 — **Shields damaged.** Reduce Defensive Value by 1.
5 — **Pulse Laser C damaged.** Reduce chance to hit by 1.
6 — **Missile Launcher C damaged.** Weapon may not fire until after next game turn.
7 — **Gunner C killed.** Lose use of Gunner C's weapons.
8 — **Structural Damage.** Take 10 more hits on this Damage Track and 8 more on the Left Side Damage Track.

## REAR CRITICAL HITS
2 — **Structural Collapse.** Hull ruptures and gunboat is lost.
3 — **Electronic Warfare gone.** Epping cannot jam torps. Reduce Defensive Value by 2.
4 — **Shields damaged.** Reduce Defensive Value by 1.
5 — **Good Hit!** Add another 5 points of damage.
6 — **Maneuver Thrusters damaged.** All turns cost 1 extra movement point.
7 — **Pilot dazed.** Epping may not move nor fire Meld Laser until after next game turn.
8 — **Reactor Hit.** Epping disappears in a ball of hot gasses.

Ship display updated in *Sunrunners*

# SCORPION

**I.D.**

**BPV: 122**

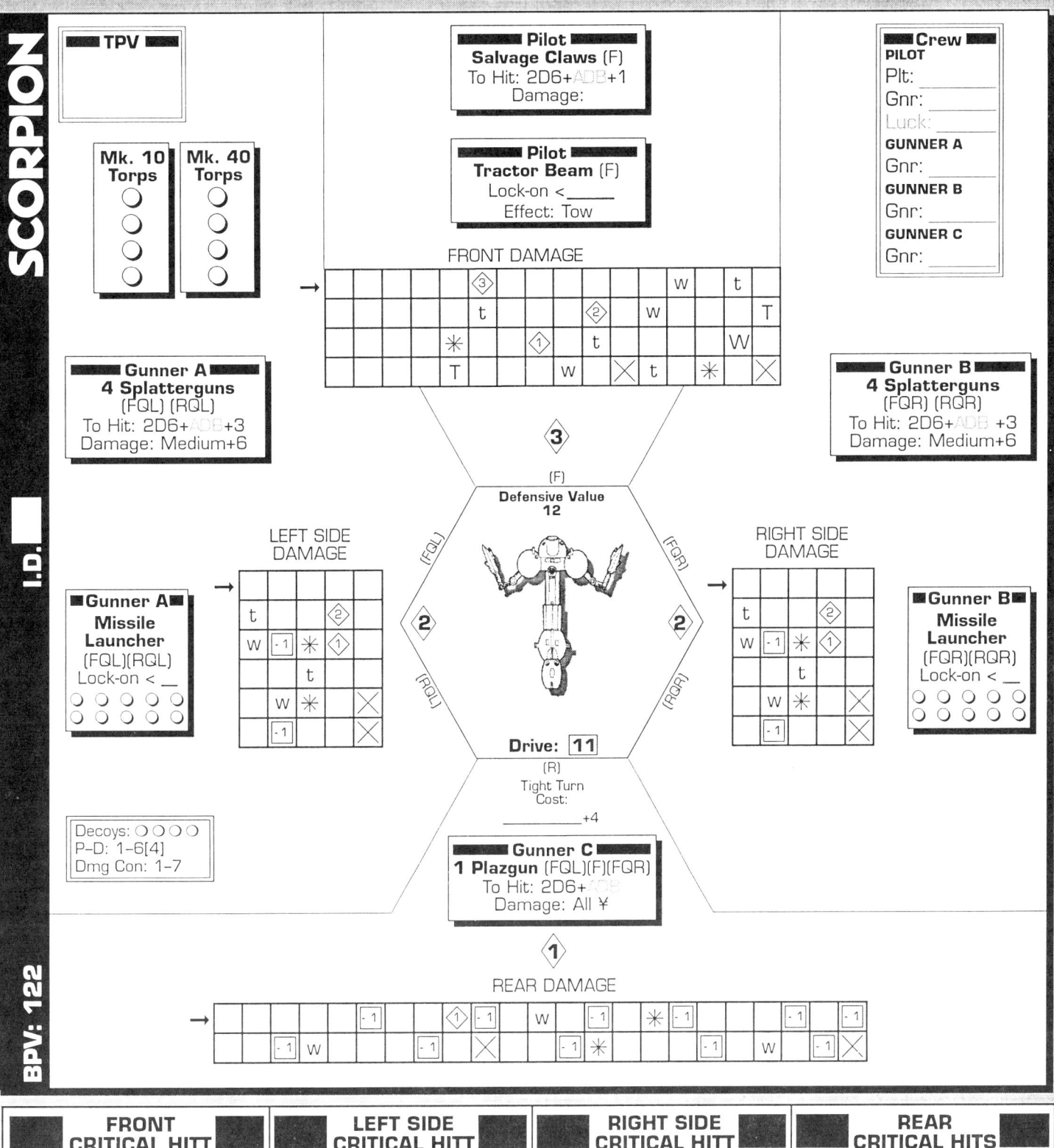

**TPV**

**Pilot**
**Salvage Claws** (F)
To Hit: 2D6+ADB+1
Damage:

**Pilot**
**Tractor Beam** (F)
Lock-on <_____
Effect: Tow

**Crew**
PILOT
Plt: _____
Gnr: _____
Luck: _____
**GUNNER A**
Gnr: _____
**GUNNER B**
Gnr: _____
**GUNNER C**
Gnr: _____

Mk. 10 Torps
Mk. 40 Torps

**Gunner A**
**4 Splatterguns**
(FQL) (RQL)
To Hit: 2D6+ADB+3
Damage: Medium+6

**Gunner B**
**4 Splatterguns**
(FQR) (RQR)
To Hit: 2D6+ADB +3
Damage: Medium+6

FRONT DAMAGE

**Gunner A**
**Missile Launcher**
(FQL)(RQL)
Lock-on < __

**Gunner B**
**Missile Launcher**
(FQR)(RQR)
Lock-on < __

LEFT SIDE DAMAGE

RIGHT SIDE DAMAGE

Defensive Value
12
(F)

(FQL)  (FQR)

3

2    2

(RQL)  (RQR)

Drive: 11
(R)
Tight Turn Cost:
_____ +4

Decoys: ○ ○ ○ ○
P–D: 1–6[4]
Dmg Con: 1–7

**Gunner C**
**1 Plazgun** (FQL)(F)(FQR)
To Hit: 2D6+ADB
Damage: All ¥

1

REAR DAMAGE

| FRONT CRITICAL HITT | LEFT SIDE CRITICAL HITT | RIGHT SIDE CRITICAL HITT | REAR CRITICAL HITS |
|---|---|---|---|
| 2 — Pilot Dazed. Scorpion may not move and Pilot may not fire until after next turn. | 2 — Gunner A killed. Those weapons may not be fired. | 2 — Gunner B killed. Those weapons may not be fired. | 2 — Gunner C killed. Plazgun may not be fired. |
| 3 — Claws damaged. Can't tow. | 3 — Missile Launcher A jams. Can't be used until after next turn. | 3 — Missile Launcher B jams. Can't be used until after next turn. | 3 — Maneuver Thrusters damaged. All turns cost one extra movement point to perform. |
| 4 — Shields damaged. Reduce Defensive Value by 1. | 4 — Shields damaged. Reduce Defensive Value by 1. | 4 — Shields damaged. Reduce Defensive Value by 1. | 4 — Shields damaged. DV –1. |
| 5 — Claws malfunction. May not be used until after next turn. | 5 — Decoy hit. Lose one decoy. | 5 — Decoy hit. Lose one decoy. | 5 — Plazgun damaged. Reduce weapon's chance to hit by 2. |
| 6 — Tractor Beam loses power. Can't use until after next turn. | 6 — Splatterguns A damaged. May not fire until after next turn. | 6 — Splatterguns B damaged. May not fire until after next turn. | 6 — Plazgun Targeter hit. May not fire until after next turn. |
| 7 — Heavy structural damage. Take 3 hits on each Damage Track. | 7 — Structural damage. Take 3 hits on both side Damage Tracks. | 7 — Structural damage. Take 3 hits on both side Damage Tracks. | 7 — Tail severely damaged. Take 10 hits on this Damage Track |
| 8 — Pilot Killed. Scorpion is at Drive 0 and Pilot's weapons are out. | 8 — Electronic Warfare knocked out. Scorp may no longer jam torps. DV –2. | 8 — Electronic Warfare knocked out. Scorp may no longer jam torps. DV –2. | 8 — Reactor detonates. Scorpion is destroyed. |

## Warhead Table

| Warhead | Attack Dice | Range | Damage |
|---|---|---|---|
| Missile | 5d6 | 1-10* | High + 5 |
| Missile | 10d6 | 1-10* | High +10 |

Missiles fire in groups of 5 or 10.

Each Missile fired add 1d6 to the attack dice and +1 to damage. The Attack Dice of the missile must meet or beat the Defensive Value of the target vessel to do any damage.

* Missile targets only need to be within 10 hexes during the Warhead launch phase. Range at impact is inconsequential.

| Warhead | Dice | Damage | Defensive Value | Speed | Alt Speed | Flak Counters |
|---|---|---|---|---|---|---|
| MK 10 Standard | 1d12 | All | 10 | 12 | 18 | - |
| MK 20 Standard | 2d12 | All | 10 | 12 | 16 | - |
| MK 30 Standard | 3d12 | All | 10 | 12 | 14 | - |
| MK 40 Standard | 4d12 | All | 10 | 12 | 12 | - |
| MK 50 Standard | 5d12 | All | 10 | 12 | 10 | - |
| MK 10 Stinger | 1d12 | ½¤ | 10 | 12 | 18 | - |
| MK 20 Stinger | 2d12 | ½¤ | 10 | 12 | 16 | - |
| MK 30 Stinger | 3d12 | ½¤ | 10 | 12 | 14 | - |
| MK 40 Stinger | 4d12 | ½¤ | 10 | 12 | 12 | - |
| MK 50 Stinger | 5d12 | ½¤ | 10 | 12 | 10 | - |
| MK 10 Venter | - | - | 8 | 12 | 18 | 2 |
| MK 20 Venter | - | - | 8 | 12 | 16 | 3 |
| MK 30 Venter | - | - | 8 | 12 | 14 | 4 |
| MK 40 Venter | - | - | 8 | 12 | 12 | 5 |
| MK 50 Venter | - | - | 8 | 12 | 10 | 6 |

¤ Stingers do half damage, ignoring Damage Reduction. If a 12 is rolled the target takes another Critical Hit in addition to normal damage

A Flak Strike is 3d6 for the initial counter, +1d6 for each additional counter. This attack must meet or beat the Defensive Value of anything passing through the flak occupied hex to do any damage. Damage for flak is High +¼ Drive

## New Weapon System Data Table

| Weapon System | Cost | Slots | Base Attack Dice | Damage | Ammo |
|---|---|---|---|---|---|
| EMP Ray | 3 | 1 | 2D8 | Medium | ∞ |
| EMP Beam | 5 | 4 | 2D8 | High | ∞ |
| Tractor Beam* | 5 | 5 | — | — | N/A |
| Salvage Claw * | 5 | 10 | 2D6 | Medium | N/A |

* Pilot only.

## Drift Table

| Current Drive | Drift Die |
|---|---|
| 0–5 | — |
| 6–10 | 1D4 |
| 11–15 | 1D6 |
| 16–19 | 1D8 |
| 20+ | 1D10 |

## Gunboats vs. Missiles Table

| Roll | Side Attacked |
|---|---|
| 1 | Front |
| 2 | Left |
| 3 | Right |
| 4-6 | Rear |

# Integrated Torpedo Table

| Torp Type | Drive | Duration | Damage Delivered | Defensive Value | Plt | Tracking Cone | Homing System | Notes |
|---|---|---|---|---|---|---|---|---|
| **Mk. 10 Torp Loads** | | | | | | | | |
| Standard Mk. 10 Torp | 12 | 10 | 1D12 | 10 | 5 | 360° | ALH | |
| Express–110 Torp | 18 | 10 | 1D12 | 10 | 3 | 360° | ALH | |
| Sentinbl–210 Torp | 12 | 10 | 1D12 | 10 | 4 | 180° | FTH | Torp remains stationary until a target is within 10 hexes at the start of a Movement Phase. |
| DFWH–310 Torp | 8/15 | 10 | 1D12 | 12 | 2 | 180° | DTH | Drive is 8 while directed or unguided Drive 15 after terminal guidance. |
| Review–410 Torp | 10 | 10 | 1D12 | 8 | 4 | 180° | CSH | |
| Relock–510 Torp | 15 | 5 | 1D12 | 11 | 2 | 180° | IFH | |
| Deadlock–610 Torp | 18 | 2 | 1D12 | 10 | 2 | 360° | IFH | |
| Remote R–10 Torp | 8 | 3 | 1D12 | 8 | 2 | — | DXH | |
| Stinger S-10 Torp | 18 | 7 | 1/2 1d12 | 10 | 4 | 360° | ALH | |
| Venter V-10 Torp | 18 | 4 | Flak | 8 | 1 | 360° | — | Disperses 2 Flak Counters. |
| **Mk. 20 Torp Loads** | | | | | | | | |
| Standard Mk. 20 Torp | 12 | 10 | 2D12 | 10 | 5 | 360° | ALH | |
| Express–120 Torp | 16 | 10 | 2D12 | 10 | 3 | 360° | ALH | |
| Review–420 Torp | 10 | 10 | 2D12 | 8 | 4 | 180° | CSH | |
| Relock–520 Torp | 14 | 5 | 2D12 | 11 | 2 | 180° | IFH | |
| Deadlock–620 Torp | 16 | 2 | 2D12 | 10 | 2 | 360° | IFH | |
| Stinger S-20 Torp | 16 | 7 | 1/2 2d12 | 10 | 4 | 360° | ALH | |
| Venter V-20 Torp | 16 | 4 | Flak | 8 | 1 | 360° | — | Disperses 3 Flak Counters. |
| **Mk. 30 Torp Loads** | | | | | | | | |
| Standard Mk. 30 Torp | 12 | 10 | 3D12 | 10 | 5 | 360° | ALH | |
| Express–130 Torp | 14 | 10 | 3D12 | 10 | 3 | 360° | ALH | |
| Sentinel–230 Torp | 12 | 10 | 3D12 | 10 | 3 | 180° | FTH | Torp remains stationary until a target is within 10 hexes at the start of a Movement Phase. |
| Relock–530 Torp | 13 | 5 | 3D12 | 11 | 2 | 180° | IFH | |
| Deadlock–630 Torp | 14 | 2 | 3D12 | 10 | 2 | 360° | IFH | |
| Remote R–30 Torp | 8 | 4 | 3D12 | 8 | 2 | — | DXH | |
| Stinger S-30 Torp | 14 | 7 | 1/2 3d12 | 10 | 4 | 360° | ALH | |
| Venter V-30 Torp | 14 | 4 | Flak | 8 | 1 | 360° | — | Disperses 4 Flak Counters. |
| **Mk. 40 Torp Loads** | | | | | | | | |
| Standard Mk. 40 Torp | 12 | 10 | 4D12 | 10 | 5 | 360° | ALH | |
| DFWH–340 Torp | 8/12 | 10 | 4D12 | 12 | 2 | 180° | DTH | Drive is 8 while directed or unguided. Drive 12 after terminal guidance. |
| Review–440 Torp | 9 | 10 | 4D12 | 9 | 4 | 180° | CSH | |
| Deadlock–640 Torp | 18 | 2 | 4D12 | 10 | 2 | 360° | IFH | |
| J40 Decoy–X Torp | 12 | 1 | — | 10 | 2 | — | DXH | Negates one decoy of the launcher's choice. |
| Stinger S-40 Torp | 12 | 7 | 1/2 4d12 | 10 | 4 | 360° | ALH | |
| Venter V-40 Torp | 12 | 4 | Flak | 8 | 1 | 360° | — | Disperses 5 Flak Counters. |
| **Mk. 50 Torp Loads** | | | | | | | | |
| Standard Mk. 50 Torp | 12 | 10 | 5D12 | 10 | 5 | 360° | ALH | |
| Ex50 (surplus) Torp | 10 | 10 | 5D12 | 10 | 2 | 60° | FTH | Only used when a scenario calls for it. |
| Relock–550 Torp | 11 | 5 | 5D12 | 11 | 2 | 180° | IFH | |
| Mayhem –750 Torp | 10 | 2 | — | 10 | 2 | — | DXH | Carries 5 Relock–510 torps. At the start of the torp's third Movement Phase, the 510s deploy in five different directions (except rear). |
| Remote R–50 Torp | 8 | 5 | 5D12 | 8 | 2 | — | DXH | |
| Stinger S-50 Torp | 10 | 7 | 1/2 5d12 | 10 | 4 | 360° | ALH | |
| Venter V-50 Torp | 10 | 4 | Flak | 8 | 1 | 360° | — | Disperses 6 Flak Counters. |

# The Next Millenium

**Torp Type:** The torp's name.

**Drive:** The number of movement point the torp must use each turn (unless it has a DXH homer–then it can spend less).

**Duration:** Number of turns the torp can move. If the torp hasn't detonated when this is over, remove it.

**Damage Delivered:** When the torp hits, roll these dice. Add them up for All damage.

**Defensive Value:** The number needed to hit the torp with an attack from a cannon or warhead.

**Plt:** The torp's Piloting skill. This is used only when the torp is trying to dodge other torps.

**Tracking Cone:** The angle through which the torp can track a target. See pages 72–73 in the SD:TNM rulebook for full details.

**Homing System:** The type of homing system the torp uses to follow its targets. See page 73 in the SD:TNM rulebook for full details.

**Notes:** Special rules for this type of torp.

# Silent Death

## Damage Track Key

▢ = Reduce the vessel's current Drive to the highest unmarked, boxed number on the damage track.

-1 = On a gunboat, the starcraft's current Drive number is reduced by 1.

◇ = Reduce the vessel's Damage Reduction to the highest unmarked diamond value on the damage track.

w = Eliminate a cannon mount or missile launcher (defender's choice).

W = Eliminate a cannon mount or missile launcher (attacker's choice).

t = Eliminate one remaining torp (defender's choice).

T = Eliminate one remaining torp (attacker's choice).

✳ = Roll 2D6 on the target vessel's Critical Hit chart. Roll 2D4 for Gunboats. Apply the critical effect immediately.

X = If this box is marked off of a fighter's display, it's destroyed. A gunboat is destroyed if two of these boxes are marked off.

C = Cargo bay hit. Cargo lost.

## Mk 50 Venter Example

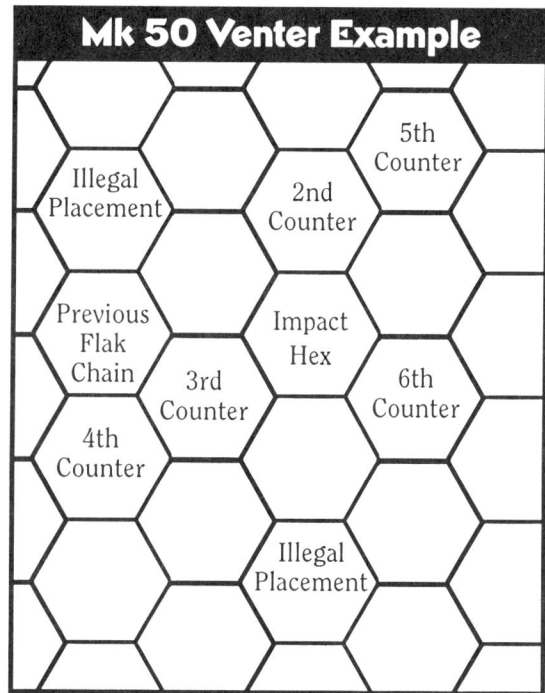

## Venter Table

| Mk | Flak | |
|---|---|---|
| 10 | 2 | Damage = High +¼DR. |
| 20 | 3 | Each additional counter |
| 30 | 4 | +1D6 to hit /+1 damage. |
| 40 | 5 | |
| 50 | 6 | |

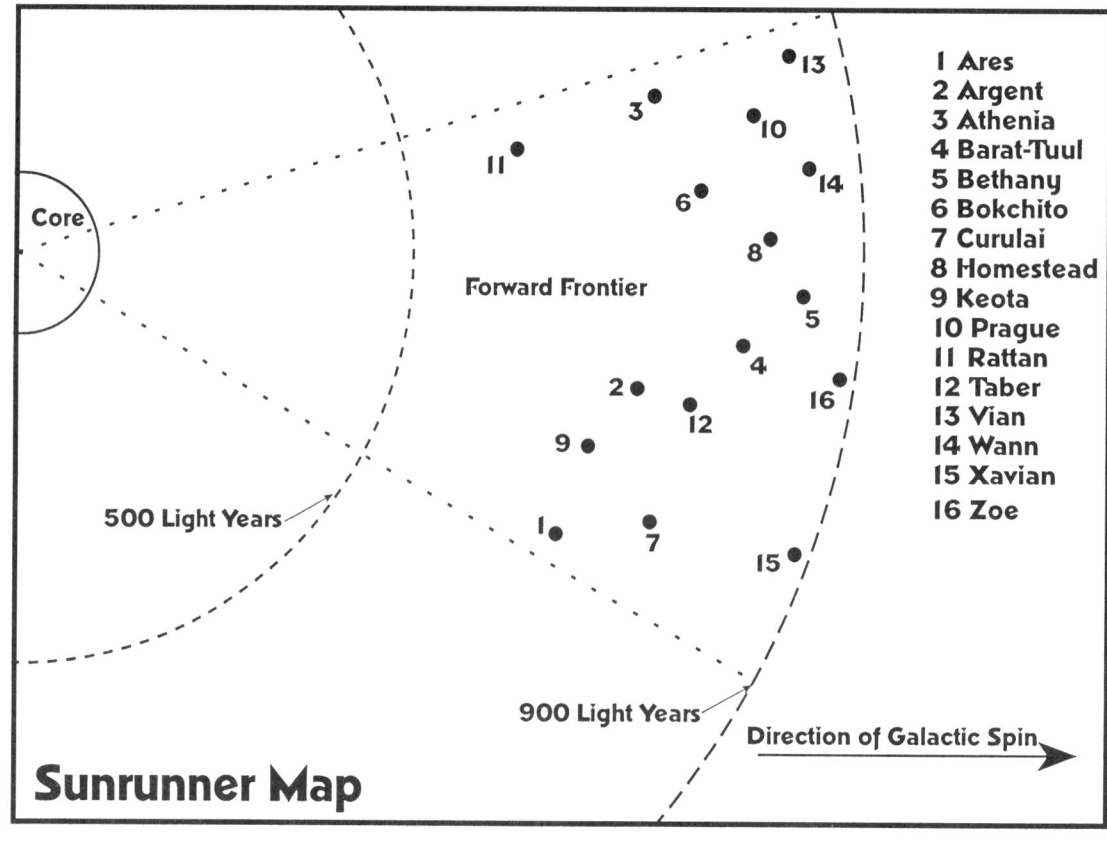

## Sunrunner Map

1 Ares
2 Argent
3 Athenia
4 Barat-Tuul
5 Bethany
6 Bokchito
7 Curulai
8 Homestead
9 Keota
10 Prague
11 Rattan
12 Taber
13 Vian
14 Wann
15 Xavian
16 Zoe

**The Next Millenium**

## WANN 36TH INTERCEPTOR GROUP
### "TOTEN TANZ"
**Commanding Officer:** Matthew Yohr

The Toten Tanz is a standard interceptor group of the Wann military. Those inhabitants still living on Wann after the exodus are the convicts, criminals, dissidents and lower classes left behind by the more powerful inhabitants. After a few years of constant internal turmoil, the Wann formed a tenuous central government in an attempt to gain a foothold in the power struggles of the new Frontier. Their success in this area has been limited and a significant portion of their military engage in piracy to supplement their income and have fun.

As a fighting force, the Wann have a lot of skill and strength, but are poor at working as a unified force. It is not unheard of for in-fighting to break out during a battle.

Typical pilot (Plt 6, Gnr 5, Lck 3)
Typical gunner (Gnr 7)

### SQUAD 1
**Squadron Leader:**
Teresa Wolfe (Plt 9, Gnr 10, Lck 2)
**Assets:** 2 x Revenge
8 x Blizzard

### SQUAD 2
**Squadron Leader:**
Danl Ver Haag (Plt 7, Gnr 8, Lck 10)
**Assets:** 2 x Revenge
8 x Hell Bender

### SQUAD 3
**Squadron Leader:**
Linus Van Vleet (Plt 6, Gnr 3, Lck 8)
**Assets:** 2 x Revenge
8 x Salamander

### SQUAD 4
**Squadron Leader:**
Raymond Moenke  (Plt 7, Gnr 4, Lck 7)
**Assets:** 2 x Revenge
8 x Teal Hawk

## INDEPENDANT PIRATE FORCE
### "WILLEM'S REVENGE"
**Commanding Officer:** Matthew Sina

Willem's Revenge is a pirate force which formed during the War. A group of traders and commercial pilots took advantage of the general chaos to extract a fortune for themselves. They became fairly successful, escaping both the Grubs and Human authorities. In the less-chaotic post-War era, they tend to remain in the outer reaches of the frontier, preying upon whoever happens along their path.

Typical pilot (Plt 5, Gnr 6, Lck 4)
Typical gunner (Gnr 6)

### SQUAD 1
**Squadron Leader:**
Karen Throne (Plt 3, Gnr 9, Lck 3)
**Assets:** 8 x Blizzard
2 x Drakar

### SQUAD 2
**Squadron Leader:**
Michael Ryba (Plt 6, Gnr 9, Lck 4)
**Assets:** 8 x Blizzard
2 x Drakar

### SQUAD 3
**Squadron Leader:**
Dane Saari (Plt 4, Gnr 4, Lck 1)
**Assets:** 8 x Blizzard
2 x Drakar

### SQUAD 4
**Squadron Leader:**
Jodi Maar (Plt 3, Gnr 6, Lck 3)
**Assets:** 8 x Blizzard
2 x Drakar

### INDEPENDENT PIRATE FORCE
#### "WILDCATS"
**Commanding Officer:** Laine Eason

The Wildcats are one of the pirate forces that existed before the War, and has survived through it. The Wildcats are selective about their targets, already having amassed a sizable fortune from past endeavors. Many of the Wildcats continue in their piracy simply for the joy of it.

Typical pilot (Plt 5, Gnr 7, Lck 5)
Typical gunner (Gnr 5)

#### SQUAD 1

**Squadron Leader:**
   Francis Lemieux   (Plt 3, Gnr 9, Lck 6)
**Assets:**   4 x Seraph
   6 x Thunderbird

#### SQUAD 2

**Squadron Leader:**
   Kory Retza (Plt 8, Gnr 7, Lck 1)
**Assets:**   4 x Teal Hawk
   4 x Salamander
   2 x Hell Bender

#### SQUAD 3

**Squadron Leader:**
   Andrea Witt (Plt 9, Gnr 6, Lck 7)
**Assets:**   4 x Talon
   2 x Pharsii II
   4 x Kosmos

#### SQUAD 4

**Squadron Leader:**
   Mark Taggart (Plt 7, Gnr 8, Lck 7)
**Assets:**   2 x Revenge
   8 x Night Hawk

# Imperial Remnant Fighter Units

### 1313TH IMPERIAL FIGHTER WING
#### "DEVIL'S LUCK"
**Commanding Officer:** Lloyd Noth

The 1313th was one of the first fighter wings to desert at the beginning of the War. Before the War, Devil's Luck had a lucrative business in the frontier as a protection agency—an ancient but effective scam. As soon as the word of War reached, them, the 1313th took full advantage of the situation. With the end of the War and the vast depletion of resources in so many systems, Devil's Luck took to actual piracy, finding it much to their liking.

Typical pilot (Plt 6, Gnr 5, Lck 3)
Typical gunner (Gnr 8)

#### SQUAD 1

**Squadron Leader:**
   Thomas Meiers (Plt 10, Gnr 9, Lck 9)
**Assets:**   4 x Pharsii II
   6 x Night Hawk

#### SQUAD 2

**Squadron Leader:**
   Lee Kita (Plt 6, Gnr 9, Lck 5)
**Assets:**   4 x Pharsii II
   6 x Night Hawk

#### SQUAD 3

**Squadron Leader:**
   David Hesse (Plt 5, Gnr 3, Lck 4)
**Assets:**   4 x Pharsii II
   6 x Night Hawk

#### SQUAD 4

**Squadron Leader:**
   Gabriel Todd (Plt 9, Gnr 6, Lck 6)
**Assets:**   4 x Pharsii II
   6 x Night Hawk

## 1968TH SPECIAL FORCES FIGHTER GROUP "NECROMANCERS"
**Commanding Officer:** Michael Reusch

The Necromancers were officially disbanded by the Emperor just prior to the onset of the War because of their gruesome tactics in dealing with the Emperor's foes. Several times, the actions of the Necromancers set off conflicts they had been sent to prevent. In the current frontier, the Necromancers are still feared for their brutality and the apparent pleasure they take in the suffering of others.

Typical pilot (Plt 7, Gnr 5, Lck 4)
Typical gunner (Gnr 6)

### SQUAD 1

**Squadron Leader:**
Lynn Pyatt (Plt 7, Gnr 4, Lck 5)
**Assets:**    6 x Salamander
4 x Thunderbird

### SQUAD 2

**Squadron Leader:**
Niles Parma (Plt 7, Gnr 8, Lck 6)
**Assets:**    6 x Salamander
4 x Thunderbird

### SQUAD 3

**Squadron Leader:**
Brian McGuire (Plt 7, Gnr 5, Lck 4)
**Assets:**    6 x Salamander
4 x Thunderbird

### SQUAD 4

**Squadron Leader:**
Chad Kane  (Plt 7, Gnr 6, Lck 4)
**Assets:**    6 x Salamander
4 x Thunderbird

## 2536TH IMPERIAL FIGHTER WING "LUCIFER'S HAMMER"
**Commanding Officer:** Carol Kanz

Lucifer's Hammer was a fighter wing which was written off by the Imperial forces. Decimated by a Grub attack, the Hammer called for reinforcements and were denied. They managed to escape the Grubs and rebuild their strength. Through a campaign of selective destruction, the now-outlaw force took what steps they could to see that any and all Imperial forces met with defeat. It is now believed that they supplement their piratical income by performing tasks for the Twelve.

Typical pilot (Plt 6, Gnr 5, Lck 3)
Typical gunner (Gnr 6)

### SQUAD 1

**Squadron Leader:**
Greg Levine (Plt 3, Gnr 5, Lck 2)
**Assets:**    2 x Revenge
6 x Pharsii II

### SQUAD 2

**Squadron Leader:**
Kay Meyhoff (Plt 7, Gnr 6, Lck 8)
**Assets:**    2 x Revenge
6 x Pharsii II

### SQUAD 3

**Squadron Leader:**
Calvin Pahl (Plt 10, Gnr 6, Lck 10)
**Assets:**    2 x Revenge
6 x Pharsii II

### SQUAD 4

**Squadron Leader:**
Allen Schoen (Plt 7, Gnr 1, Lck 7)
**Assets:**    2 x Revenge
6 x Pharsii II

# Silent Death

# Scenarios

The 12 scenarios in this book are set up to be run in two different ways. Some of them are encounters between the Sunrunners and another force, while the remaining ones ally Sunrunner forces with those of their employers. Players may chose to ignore this ally and use small Sunrunner units, or make use of it and have a slightly larger and more spread-out battle. The inclusion of the allied forces is useful if more than two players are involved.

Several of the scenarios are divided into 2 or more battles. These are often listed as being consecutive. If the number of battles and record keeping seems a little daunting, feel free to ignore any of the later battles of a scenario. Play battle 1, or 1 and 2, and let the rest go. These consecutive battles are included for those players who enjoy a sense of continuity and extended scenarios. If you decide to play all the battles in a scenario, the salvaging of ships is done at the end of the full scenario.

In a number of battles, there are cargo ships or shuttles in the area which need to be protected by the Sunrunners or their allies. A standard form for these ships is provided with the ship sheets. To represent these ships on the playing surface, take an unused counter (for any ship) and place it face down on the map, marking a C on those which are cargo ships and an S for those which are shuttles.

All scenarios use the Luck optional rule. Half (round up) of the Sunrunner tirps must be Venters. Standard payloads are listed under starcraft nomenclature, but players may choose different loads.

# Scenario 1: "Plugging the Leak"

The Keota have hired the Sunrunners to find and destroy smugglers who were involved with a data leak. The smuggler ships have met to exchange information and resources when they are attacked by elements of Windclaw's North squadron.

## Forces

### Windclaw Elements from the North Squad. (TPV: 239)

**Commanding Officer**:
Gregor Radekt (Windjammer)

Set up first along edge 1.

Windjammer A—   Pilot (Plt 8, Gnr 10, Lck 7)
Windjammer B—   Pilot (Plt 7, Gnr 4, Lck 1)
Wavecutter A—   Pilot (Plt 8, Gnr 5, Lck 1)
Wavecutter B—   Pilot (Plt 7, Gnr 4, Lck 1)
Salamander A—   Pilot (Plt 8, Gnr 4, Lck 1)
                Gunner A (Gnr 6)

### Smugglers (TPV: 239)

Set up second in sections E & F within 7 hexes of each other.

Hell Bender A—   Pilot (Plt 8, Gnr 9, Lck 5)
Hell Bender B—   Pilot (Plt 7, Gnr 7, Lck 1)
Hell Bender C—   Pilot (Plt 5, Gnr 6)
Spirit Rider A—   Pilot (Plt 7, Gnr 7, Lck 3)
Spirit Rider B—   Pilot (Plt 6, Gnr 6, Lck 1)
Spirit Rider C—   Pilot (Plt 6, Gnr 5)

## Special rules

1) Sunrunners automatically gain initiative the first turn.

2) All Sunrunner MK10 torps are Venters.

3) The Sunrunner MK20 torp is a Stinger.

4) Smugglers may flee the map on edge 3 on turn 6. These do not count as destroyed ships for Sunrunners.

## Victory Conditions

At the end of six turns Sunrunner reinforcements arrive. At that time both sides total up the TPV of all enemy starcraft destroyed. The side with the highest total wins.

## The Standard Map Setup

```
                    Edge 2
         ┌─────────────┬─────────────┐
         │      │      │      │       │
         │      │      │      │       │
  Edge 1 │──────┼──────┼──────┼────── │ Edge 3
         │      │      │      │       │
         │      │      │      │       │
         └─────────────┴─────────────┘
                    Edge 4
```

# The Next Millenium

## Death of a God

The founder and first admiral of the Sunrunners, Michael "Odin" Bach, came to be revered in his lifetime as a man of almost mythical proportions. His death was one fitting such a man. In the last days of the Empire, the Sunrunners often fought against the forces of the Emperor, both in the skies and on the ground. One such ground battle took place on a small moon in the Coriass system in the leeward edge of the Empire's reach. Racing to reach their ships, the Emperor's shock troops charging at their backs, the mercenaries reached the Carrier Gorge and it's only bridge, the Jhenenshire. Beyond lay their ships and the means of destroying their attackers. taking a rear-guard position, Admiral Bach sent his men across the bridge. Then, with a

# Scenario 2: "Freight Fight"

rifle in each hand, the man held his position against the advancing soldiers, slaying them as they filtered through to the narrow entrance of the bridge. At last though, the man succumbed to the wounds he had taken, and fell dead amidst the many he had slain. Taking to the air, the Sunrunner ships secured their vengeance against the troops on the ground and their superiors in the skies above, leaving not a single one alive.

The Sunrunners are escorting a Kashmere Cargo transport carrying Sunrunner scrap back to Kashmere for trade. Some local pirates have decided to grab the prize.

## Forces

### Windclaw South (TPV: 250)

Set up first in sections E & F within 9 hexes of each other, all fighters pointing in one direction.

| | |
|---|---|
| Windjammer A— | Pilot (Plt 7, Gnr 9, Lck 5) |
| Windjammer C— | Pilot (Plt 7, Gnr 5, Lck 1) |
| Wavecutter A- | Pilot (Plt 8, Gnr 5, Lck 1) |
| Wavecutter B- | Pilot (Plt 6, Gnr 6, Lck 1) |
| Havok A— | Pilot (Plt 6, Gnr 5, Lck 2) |
| | Gunner A (Gnr 7) |
| Blizzard A— | Pilot (Plt 8, Gnr 4, Lck 1) |
| Freighter A— | Pilot (Plt 4) |
| Freighter B— | Pilot (Plt 4) |

### Pirates (TPV: 248)

Set up second along edge 3.

| | |
|---|---|
| Night Hawk A— | Pilot (Plt 8, Gnr 5, Lck 4) |
| Night Hawk B— | Pilot (Plt 6, Gnr 4) |
| Galive A— | Pilot (Plt 5, Gnr 6, Lck 2) |
| | Gunner A (Gnr 8) |

## Special rules

1) The pirates gain initiative the first turn.

2) This scenario lasts 10 turns

3) All Sunrunner torps are Ventors.

4) Pirate vessels may flee the map on edge 3 on any turn after they have lost a ship. Ships that have left the board do not count as destroyed ships for Sunrunners, and may not return.

## Scoring

Any Sunrunner with at least half of its boxes and a weapon that exits the map (off edge 3) in pursuit of fleeing pirate vessels gains 15 points.

Pirates receive 50 pts for each freighter reduced to drive 0 if they still have ships on the map at the end of turn 10.

No points are awarded for destruction of the freighters Sunrunners may fire on a freighter after turn 7 if its drive is 0

## Victory Conditions

At the end of the scenario both sides total up the TPV of all enemy starcraft destroyed and any other modifiers The side with the highest total wins.

# Scenario 3: "Ghost Salvage"

The Sunrunners are claiming salvage on a small Imperium ghost fleet in orbit around a ruined world. Another group of salvage miners dispute the claim, thinking themselves safe because they are in orbit near a Brood world. The Barat decide to take the chance and try to rout the claim jumpers before the Brood awaken.

## Forces

### South (TPV: 386)

Set up first along edge 1.

| | |
|---|---|
| Windjammer A— | Pilot (Plt 7, Gnr 9, Lck 5) |
| Windjammer B— | Pilot (Plt 8, Gnr 4, Lck 1) |
| Windjammer C— | Pilot (Plt 7, Gnr 5, Lck 1) |
| Wavecutter A— | Pilot (Plt 8, Gnr 4, Lck 1) |
| Wavecutter B— | Pilot (Plt 6, Gnr 6, Lck 1) |
| Havok A— | Pilot (Plt 6, Gnr 5, Lck 1) |
| | Gunner A (Gnr 7) |
| Havok B— | Pilot (Plt 7, Gnr 5, Lck 1) |
| | Gunner A (Gnr 6) |
| Blizzard A— | Pilot (Plt 8, Gnr 4, Lck 1) |
| Blizzard B— | Pilot (Plt 7, Gnr 5, Lck 1) |

### Claim Jumpers (TPV: 386)

Set up Second within 6 hexes of edge 3

| | |
|---|---|
| Lance Electra A— | Pilot (Plt 7, Gnr 9, Lck 1) |
| | Gunner A (Gnr 8) |
| Lance Electra B— | Pilot (Plt 8, Gnr 4) |
| | Gunner A (Gnr 5) |
| Night Hawk A— | Pilot (Plt 7, Gnr 4) |
| Talon A— | Pilot (Plt 6, Gnr 5) |
| Talon B— | Pilot (Plt 7, Gnr 5) |
| Pit Viper A— | Pilot (Plt 8, Gnr 4) |
| Pit Viper B— | Pilot (Plt 7, Gnr 5) |
| Pit Viper C— | Pilot (Plt 7, Gnr 5) |

## Special Rules

1) Scatter 20 asteroids or unused ships around the map to represent the ghost fleet. These are dead ships and space rubble. They do not block line of site for any targeting, but will do 3d6 low to anything moving through a hex so marked. They do not drift.

2) Sunrunner ships only have Stinger Torps.

3) Claim jumpers may flee the board at any time, Sunrunners may not.

4) Sunrunners may surrender or accept surrender on turn ten.

## Victory Conditions

Whichever side holds the board at the end of turn ten wins unless both lose.

If one side does not surrender to the other before the end of turn 10, both sides lose because the Brood awakens and swarms.

# Scenario 4: "Barbarians at the Gate"

*"We've lost seven shipments this last cycle. Some we saved and can ship later, but that doesn't help any." Brigid Rielly sat back in the plush chair, a look of exasperation on her face. "We've got some damn fine fighters out there, but those women are getting tired. And these pirates have newer ships and more fire power than we can afford to match."*

*"Can you afford us?" The harsh gutturals of Jacob Bach's accent complemented Reilly's rolling brogue.*

*"You say you'll take payment in trade?"*

*"If it's something we can use, yes. As long as a fair value is set for it." Jacob took another look at the woman in front of him. He had liked her from the first—strong willed, confident, intelligent and, admittedly, quite beautiful in a way that appealed to Jacob. She was a warrior like himself, though now relegated to a position in the political arena. "What kind of a force are we talking about?"*

*"They're running four squads of ten ships each. So far, it's only been one or two squads at a time at one place, but they've been known to hit four different places at once. What I want is a force of sufficient strength to eliminate these scoundrels once and for all."*

*A wicked smile emerged on Jacob's face. "No raider left alive?"*

*"Not a single one." This woman was becoming even more attractive. "And I've been authorized to offer a bonus if you can accomplish it within a few guidelines."*

*"Name them."*

## Battle I

**Date:** AL 9:023

**Location:** Low orbit above Bethany.

**Situation:** One squad of the pirate force "Willem's Revenge" has entered Bethan orbit with the intention of raiding an orbital docking station for recreational drugs to sell on the black and open markets at prices below those of the Bethans. It comes in from behind Bethany's moon at high speeds. It is the objective of the Sunrunner force to protect the docking facility from attack and eliminate any and all pirate ships.

## Forces

### Sunrunners: Jacob's Thunder, North (TPV: 321)

Set up in area E (Standard Map Setup).

| | |
|---|---|
| Wavecutter A— | Pilot (Plt 9, Gnr 6, Lck 10) |
| Wavecutter B— | Pilot (Plt 8, Gnr 6, Lck 2) |
| Hellbender A— | Pilot (Plt 8, Gnr 7, Lck 2) |
| Night Hawk A— | Pilot (Plt 7, Gnr 6, Lck 2) |
| Death Wind A— | Pilot (Plt 8, Gnr 6, Lck 2) |
| | Gunner A (Gnr 9) |
| Spirit Rider A— | Pilot (Plt 8, Gnr 6, Lck 2) |

### Elements from Bethan 82nd Defensive Group. Manslayers Squadron 1 (TPV: 225)

Setup in Area G (Standard Map)

| | |
|---|---|
| Salamander C— | Pilot (Plt 7, Gnr 6/Gnr 7) |
| Revenge A— | Pilot (Plt 8, Gnr 1, Lck 3) |
| | Gunner A (Gnr 7) |

### Independent Pirate Force Willem's Revenge Squadron 1 (TPV: 562)

**Commanding Officer:** Karen Thorne

Setup Second in area B (Standard Map)

| | |
|---|---|
| Blizzard A— | Pilot (Plt 8, Gnr 6) |
| Blizzard B— | Pilot (Plt 7, Gnr 5) |
| Blizzard C— | Pilot (Plt 6, Gnr 6) |
| Blizzard D— | Pilot (Plt 6, Gnr 5) |
| Blizzard E— | Pilot (Plt 6, Gnr 5) |
| Blizzard F— | Pilot (Plt 5, Gnr 4) |
| Blizzard G— | Pilot (Plt 4, Gnr 7) |
| Blizzard H— | Pilot (Plt 3, Gnr 1) |
| Drakar A— | Pilot (Plt 7, Gnr 5, Lck 4) |
| | Gunner A (Gnr 7) |
| | Gunner B (Gnr 7) |
| | Gunner C (Gnr 7) |
| | Gunner D (Gnr 6) |

Drakar B—    Pilot (Plt 6, Gnr 6, Lck3)
             Gunner A (Gnr 8)
             Gunner B (Gnr 6)
             Gunner C (Gnr 6)
             Gunner D (Gnr 6)

Set up by the Willem's Revenge player in areas E, F and H, no more than 2 cargo ships per section. (sheets for the Borax Freighter and Curtis shuttle used in these scenarios are provided in the ship sheet section)

Borax Freighter A— Pilot (Plt 6)
Borax Freighter B— Pilot (Plt 6)
Borax Freighter C— Pilot (Plt 5)
Borax Freighter D— Pilot (Plt 5)
Borax Freighter E— Pilot (Plt 4)
Borax Freighter F— Pilot (Plt 4)

**Station:** Placed randomly in area G

## Special Rules

1) Beyond edge 4 is Bethany. The last two rows of hexes along edge 4 represent the upper atmosphere of the planet. For those ships with atmospheric capability, diving into the atmosphere (including exiting edge 4) is allowed.

2) Any ship with more than 1/2 of it's damage track marked upon entering the atmosphere must roll 1d6. If the result is a 1, the ship takes 1d6 points of damage from atmospheric impact. This is straight damage, no damage reductions is applied to this damage.

3) Pirate ships may leave the playing area without penalty. Once they have left, they may not return to play.

4) There are 6 Borax Freighters at and around the docking facility. These ships have no offensive capabilities, and are under the protection of the defending forces. [Note: if the Bethan forces are used, they must be reserved for the protection of the cargo ships, and can not actively pursue combat with the pirates otherwise.]

5) The freighters move before all other ships and are moved by the Sunrunner player. They may leave the map thru section A on edge 1 or 2. If this is done they have escaped the attack.

6) The Station has no offensive capabilities of its own. The pirates will not attack the station, they need it intact.

## Victory Conditions

The battle is over when all pirate ships are either destroyed or have fled, or all Sunrunner Bethany ships are destroyed or disabled. At the end of the game , both sides total up the TPV of all enemy starcraft destroyed. Both sides should check to see if there eligible for any extra Points against the list below. The side with the highest total wins. A tie result indicates a draw.

## Sunrunner & Bethany
## Bonus Points

+10 for every Pirate fled
+15 for every freighter undamaged at the end of play
- 40 for using the Bethan forces in the scenario

## Willem's Revenge
## Bonus Points

+10 for every Bethan ship fled
+15 for every freighter destroyed or disabled

# Battle 2

**Date:** AL 9:023
**Location:** High orbit over Bethany
**Situation:** A second force of pirates is advancing to attack a fueling depot in high orbit over Bethany's magnetic north pole. The Sunrunners intercept them just out of range of the depot.

## Forces:

### Sunrunners: Jacob's Thunder West (TPV: 567)

Set up along edge 4 (Standard Map Setup).

Sorenson III A—    Pilot (Plt 9, Gnr 7, Lck 4)
                   Gunner A (Gnr 7)
Sorenson III B—    Pilot (Plt 8, Gnr 6, Lck 2)
                   Gunner A (Gnr 6)
Sorenson III C—    Pilot (Plt 7, Gnr 6, Lck, 2)
                   Gunner A (Gnr 6)
Sorenson III D—    Pilot (Plt 8, Gnr 5, Lck 2)
                   Gunner A (Gnr 5)
Salamander A—      Pilot (Plt 8, Gnr 7, Lck 2)
                   Gunner A (Gnr 9)
Wavecutter A—      Pilot (Plt 8, Gnr 6, Lck 2)
Wavecutter B—      Pilot (Plt 7, Gnr 5, Lck 2)
Thunderbird A—     Pilot (Plt 5, Gnr 7, Lck 2)

# The Next Millenium

# Silent Death

## Independent Pirate Force Willem's Revenge, Squadron 2 (TPV: 562)

Set up along edge 2 (Standard Map Setup).

| | |
|---|---|
| Blizzard A— | Pilot(Plt 7, Gnr 6) |
| Blizzard B— | Pilot(Plt 7, Gnr 5) |
| Blizzard C— | Pilot(Plt 6, Gnr 6) |
| Blizzard D— | Pilot(Plt 6, Gnr 5) |
| Blizzard E— | Pilot(Plt 6, Gnr 5) |
| Blizzard F— | Pilot(Plt 5, Gnr 4) |
| Blizzard G— | Pilot(Plt 5, Gnr 5) |
| Blizzard H— | Pilot(Plt 3, Gnr 3) |
| Drakar A— | Pilot(Plt 7, Gnr 5, Lck 4) |
| | Gunner A (Gnr 8) |
| | Gunner B (Gnr 6) |
| | Gunner C (Gnr 7) |
| | Gunner D (Gnr 7) |
| Drakar B— | Pilot(Plt 6, Gnr 6, Lck 3) |
| | Gunner A (Gnr 7) |
| | Gunner B (Gnr 7) |
| | Gunner C (Gnr 6) |
| | Gunner D (Gnr 5) |

## Special Rules

**1)** Pirate ships may leave the playing area without penalty. Once they have left, they may not return to play.

## Victory Conditions

The battle is over when all ships on one side have been destroyed or disabled or have left the playing surface. Pirate ships which leave the playing surface are considered to have fled. They are not destroyed, but may not return to play. At the end of the game, both sides total up the TPV of all enemy starcraft destroyed. Both sides should check to see if they are eligible for any extra Points against the list below. The side with the highest total wins. A tie result indicates a draw.

## Sunrunner Bonus Points

+10 for every Pirate fled

## Willem's Revenge Bonus Points

+10 for every Sunrunner ship fled

# Battle 3

**Date:** AL 9:025

**Location:** High orbit above Bethany

**Situation:** The last of the pirate force of Willem's Revenge are in need of fuel and supplies. The two squads remaining form a two-pronged attack against the main pharmaceutical refinery and supply station at LaGrange point 1 (at the gravitic midway of Bethany and Dio). Force one enters the battle from behind the moon; force two, from high orbit around Bethany. The Sunrunners and the second half of the Manslayers are a short distance out from the station to intercept.

## Forces

### Flank A

#### Sunrunners: Jacob's Thunder (TPV: 458)

Setup [A-Flank] in areas C & D (Long Map Setup).

| | |
|---|---|
| Night Hawk A— | Pilot (Plt 9, Gnr 7, Lck 4) |
| Sorenson III A— | Pilot (Plt 8, Gnr 6, Lck 2) |
| | Gunner A (Gnr 6) |
| Hellbender A— | Pilot (Plt 8, Gnr 7, Lck 2) |
| Havok A— | Pilot (Plt 8, Gnr 6, Lck 2) |
| | Gunner A (Gnr 9) |
| Salamander A— | Pilot (Plt 8, Gnr 7, Lck 2) |
| | Gunner A (Gnr 9) |
| Wavecutter A— | Pilot (Plt 8, Gnr 6, Lck 2) |
| Wavecutter B— | Pilot (Plt 7, Gnr 5, Lck 2) |

#### Willem's Revenge Squadron 3 (TPV: 554)

Setup [A-Flank] in areas A & B (Long Map Setup).

| | |
|---|---|
| Blizzard A— | Pilot (Plt 6, Gnr 7) |
| Blizzard B— | Pilot (Plt 6, Gnr 6) |
| Blizzard C— | Pilot (Plt 6, Gnr 5) |
| Blizzard D— | Pilot (Plt 5, Gnr 6) |
| Blizzard E— | Pilot (Plt 5, Gnr 5) |
| Blizzard F— | Pilot (Plt 5, Gnr 5) |
| Blizzard G— | Pilot (Plt 4, Gnr 5) |
| Blizzard H— | Pilot (Plt 3, Gnr 2) |
| Drakar A— | Pilot (Plt 6, Gnr 5, Lck 4) |
| | Gunner A (Gnr 7) |
| | Gunner B (Gnr 5) |
| | Gunner C (Gnr 7) |
| | Gunner D (Gnr 7) |
| Drakar B— | Pilot (Plt 6, Gnr 6, Lck 3) |
| | Gunner A (Gnr 6) |
| | Gunner A (Gnr 7) |
| | Gunner A (Gnr 5) |
| | Gunner A (Gnr 5) |

## Flank B

### Sunrunners: Jacob's Thunder
### (TPV: 408)

Setup [B-Flank] in areas E & F (Long Map Setup).

| | |
|---|---|
| Wavecutter A— | Pilot (Plt 9, Gnr 6, Lck 5) |
| Wavecutter B— | Pilot (Plt 8, Gnr 6, Lck 2) |
| Hellbender A— | Pilot (Plt 8, Gnr 7, Lck 2) |
| Night Hawk A— | Pilot (Plt 7, Gnr 6, Lck 2) |
| Salamander A— | Pilot (Plt 8, Gnr 6, Lck 2) |
| | Gunner A (Gnr 9) |
| Havok A— | Pilot (Plt 8, Gnr 7, Lck 2) |
| | Gunner A (Gnr 7) |
| Thunderbird A— | Pilot (Plt 8, Gnr 6, Lck 2) |

### Willem's Revenge Squadron 4
### (TPV: 663)

Setup [B-Flank] in areas G & H (Long Map Setup).

| | |
|---|---|
| Blizzard A— | Pilot (Plt 6, Gnr 7) |
| Blizzard B— | Pilot (Plt 6, Gnr 6) |
| Blizzard C— | Pilot (Plt 6, Gnr 5) |
| Blizzard D— | Pilot (Plt 5, Gnr 6) |
| Blizzard E— | Pilot (Plt 5, Gnr 5) |
| Blizzard F— | Pilot (Plt 4, Gnr 5) |
| Drakar A— | Pilot (Plt 6, Gnr 6, Lck 4) |
| | Gunner A (Gnr 6) |
| | Gunner B (Gnr 5) |
| | Gunner C (Gnr 6) |
| | Gunner D (Gnr 7) |
| Drakar B— | Pilot (Plt 6, Gnr 5, Lck 2) |
| | Gunner A (Gnr 6) |
| | Gunner B(Gnr 7) |
| | Gunner C (Gnr 6) |
| | Gunner D (Gnr 5) |
| Drakar C— | Pilot (Plt 5, Gnr 5 ) |
| | Gunner A (Gnr 6) |
| | Gunner B (Gnr 6) |
| | Gunner C (Gnr 5) |
| | Gunner D (Gnr 6) |

### Bethan 82nd Defensive Group
### Manslayers, Elements from Squadron 1,
### (TPV: 196)

**Commanding Officer:** Katriana Kelly

Bethan forces will be divided to defend on both fronts. Surrounding the station, facing outward. (Long Map Setup)

| | |
|---|---|
| Revenge B— | Pilot (Plt 7, Gnr 1/Gnr 6) |
| Spirit Rider A— | Pilot (Plt 8, Gnr 7) |
| Spirit Rider B— | Pilot (Plt 6, Gnr 5) |

**Station:** Centered on the map

## Special Rules

1) Reinforcements: After the 8th turn, any ships in fighting condition that are left from the previous two battles may enter the playing field at edge 1 of area E and join the battle.

2) The Bethan forces remain closer to the station and keep its defense as their main priority. Due to previous raids, the station has no weapons systems of its own.

3) The station has 6 defensive areas—corresponding to the sides of its hex—each able to take 100 points of damage before being considered out of commission. It has a damage reduction of 6, and a defensive value of 5. Once 2 of these sections are reduced to 0 the station explodes!

4) Any ship may change from A-flank to B-flank or vice-versa at any point in the battle. Sunrunners may also fall back to aid the Manslayers in the defense of the station if so desired.

5) Any pirate ship leaving the playing surface is considered to have fled and may not return to play.

## Victory Conditions:

The battle is over when all ships on one side have been destroyed or disabled or have left the playing surface. Pirate ships which leave the playing surface are considered to have fled. They are not destroyed, but may not return to play. At the end of the game, both sides total up the TPV of all enemy starcraft destroyed. Both sides should check to see if there eligible for any extra Points against the list below. The side with the highest total wins. A tie result indicates a draw.

## Sunrunner & Bethany
## Bonus Points

+10 for every Pirate fled
- 50 for using the Bethan forces in the scenario

## Willem's Revenge
## Bonus Points

+10 for every Bethan ship fled
+20 for each station zone destroyed
+120 for station destruction

## Festival of the Return

Each year, on the anniversary of the fall of Barat-Tuul, the Sunrunners remember it with the Festival of the Return. The three days of the festival are separated into the Remembrance, the Mourning, and the Conquest. Remembrance is a day for the telling of ancient tales of heroes and monsters; of reveling in the glory and pride of being Barat. The Mourning is a solemn day spent in prayer and reflection. It is a day to honor the dead and remember the pain it means to be Barat. The last day, the Conquest, is a day to look to the future, to the retaking of Barat-Tuul and the glory that will be the new Barat nation. It's a day of boasting, fighting and drunken revelry.

# Scenario 5: "The Hounds of Hell"

*"Sir, incoming fighters."*
*"You have a fix on their location?"*
*"Yes, sir."*
*"Let me see it on tactical." The glowing images appeared in the tank of the map display in front of Captain Bach. "Damn."*

*For the past three weeks, the* Maelstrom *had been tailed by a group of fighters. They never attacked, keeping on the edge of sensor range, but followed as the* Maelstrom *progressed from system to system. Now, it seemed, they were getting bolder.*

*"Lieutenant, check for any other ships in range. There's some missing from this group. I want to know where they are, and who we have to send against them. It's time we finish this game."*

## Battle 1

**Date:** AL 9:073
**Location:** Near Homestead
**Situation:** A flight of former Imperial fighters—now pirates—has followed the *Maelstrom* to it's present location. While the carrier waits to rendezvous with the Stormbringer squadron near Homestead, the pirates attack. The first attack is aimed at the Windclaw squadron after a training exercise just outside a nearby asteroid field.
[Note: Because the Sunrunners are not under contract with anyone for these battles, no KILL BONUS is awarded. Salvage occurs as normal.]

## Forces

### Sunrunners: Wind Claw, East, (TPV: 414)

Set up in area C facing direction 1

| | |
|---|---|
| Windjammer A— | Pilot (Plt 9, Gnr 7, Lck 5) |
| Wavecutter A— | Pilot (Plt 8, Gnr 4, Lck 1) |
| Wavecutter B— | Pilot (Plt 6, Gnr 6, Lck 1) |
| Salamander A— | Pilot (Plt 8, Gnr 4, Lck 1) |
| | Gunner A (Gnr 6) |
| Salamander B— | Pilot (Plt 7, Gnr 5, Lck 1) |
| | Gunner A (Gnr 6) |
| Thunderbird A— | Pilot (Plt 8, Gnr 4, Lck 1) |
| Thunderbird B— | Pilot (Plt 7, Gnr 4, Lck 1) |
| Teal Hawk A— | Pilot (Plt 7, Gnr 3, Lck 1) |
| | Gunner A (Gnr 7) |

### Pirates: Necromancers, (TPV: 686)

Set up in area H facing direction 1

| | |
|---|---|
| Salamander A— | Pilot (Plt 9, Gnr 7, Lck 5) |
| | Gunner A (Gnr 8) |
| Salamander B— | Pilot (Plt 8, Gnr 8, Lck 5) |
| | Gunner A (Gnr 9) |
| Salamander C— | Pilot (Plt 7, Gnr 6, Lck 3) |
| | Gunner A (Gnr 7) |
| Salamander D— | Pilot (Plt 6, Gnr 8, Lck 2) |
| | Gunner A (Gnr 8) |
| Salamander E— | Pilot (Plt 6, Gnr 7) |
| | Gunner A (Gnr 7) |
| Salamander F— | Pilot (Plt 5, Gnr 5) |
| | Gunner A (Gnr 6) |
| Thunderbird A— | Pilot (Plt 7, Gnr 8, Lck 5()) |
| Thunderbird B— | Pilot (Plt 7, Gnr 4, Lck 2) |
| Thunderbird C— | Pilot (Plt 6, Gnr 6) |
| Thunderbird D— | Pilot (Plt 5, Gnr 3) |

Randomly spread 20 asteroids on the Sunrunner's half of the board.

## Special Rules

1) If the number of pirate ships reaches 8 or less, they may retreat. When the number of pirate ships falls below 8, roll 1d8. If the roll is higher than the number of pirate ships, the remainder turn and flee. Each time another pirate ship is disabled or destroyed, roll again.

2) Pirate ships are allowed to leave the playing surface, but in doing so, they are considered to have fled and can not return to play.

## Victory Conditions

The battle lasts 20 turns or until all ships of one side are disabled or destroyed, or the pirate forces flee (see special rule #1).

+15 for each pirate ship disabled or destroyed
+5 for each pirate ship fled
-10 for each Sunrunner ship disabled or destroyed
-5 for each Sunrunner ship fled

# Scenario 6: "To The Victor"

Toten Tanz. On ancient, plague-ridden Earth, the Toten Tanz was the dance of death—an energetic, often hysterical dance of those driven mad by the air of death around them. To some, it was a means of preventing the disease. To others, it was an affirmation of it. It became, however, one of the ways in which the plague spread, the dancers spinning through the streets of the towns, their plague-ridden bodies passing among the masses. They danced until they died. And the question was often raised: Is there an end to the Toten Tanz? Can it be stopped?

## Battle 1

**Date:** AL 9:104
**Location:** Beta outpost in the Wann system
**Situation:** Prague needs the forces of the Beta outpost to be destroyed in order to advance upon the planets of the system, but is prevented from sending in its forces by a treaty. Using a loophole in the treaty, Prague has hired the Sunrunners to take out the outpost for it.

## Forces

### Sunrunners: God's Frost, North flight (TPV: 928)

Set up in area H.

| | |
|---|---|
| Talon A— | Pilot (Plt 9, Gnr 7, Lck 5) |
| Talon B— | Pilot (Plt 6, Gnr 5, Lck 3) |
| Spider A— | Pilot (Plt 7, Gnr 5, Lck 3) |
| | Gunner A (Gnr 8) |
| | Gunner B (Gnr 7) |
| Spider B— | Pilot (Plt 6, Gnr 5, Lck 2) |
| | Gunner A (Gnr 6) |
| | Gunner B (Gnr 6) |
| Seraph A— | Pilot (Plt 6, Gnr 5, Lck 2) |
| | Gunner A (Gnr 8) |
| Catastrophe A— | Pilot (Plt 7, Gnr 6, Lck 3) |
| | Gunner A (Gnr 7) |
| | Gunner B (Gnr 7) |
| | Gunner C (Gnr 7) |
| Havok A— | Pilot(Plt 5, Gnr 6, Lck 3) |
| | Gunner A (Gnr 9) |
| Sentry A— | Pilot(Plt 7, Gnr 6, Lck 2) |
| | Gunner A (Gnr 7) |
| | Gunner B (Gnr 7) |

### Wann: Toten Tanz, Squad 3 (TPV: 947)

Set up in area A.

| | |
|---|---|
| Salamander A— | Pilot (Plt 9, Gnr 10, Lck 9) |
| | Gunner A (Gnr 10) |
| Salamander B— | Pilot (Plt 8, Gnr 9, Lck 6) |
| | Gunner A (Gnr 9) |
| Salamander C— | Pilot (Plt 8, Gnr 7, Lck 5) |
| | Gunner A (Gnr 8) |
| Salamander D— | Pilot (Plt 7, Gnr 8, Lck 4) |
| | Gunner A (Gnr 9) |
| Salamander E— | Pilot (Plt 7, Gnr 6, Lck 4) |
| | Gunner A (Gnr 7) |
| Salamander F— | Pilot (Plt 6, Gnr 8, Lck 4) |
| | Gunner A (Gnr 8) |
| Salamander G— | Pilot (Plt 6, Gnr 7, Lck 4) |
| | Gunner A (Gnr 7) |
| Salamander H— | Pilot (Plt 6, Gnr 5, Lck 4) |
| | Gunner A (Gnr 6) |
| Revenge A— | Plt 8, Gnr 6, Lck 9 |
| | Gunner A (Gnr 8) |
| Revenge B— | Plt 7, Gnr 8, Lck 5 |
| | Gunner A (Gnr 7) |

## Special Rules

1) Due to the danger of waking one of the several nearby Clutchworlds, no torps over Mk. 20 may be used.

## Victory Conditions

The battle lasts for 7 turns. The Sunrunners win if the Wann forces are reduced to less than half of their original number of ships. At that point, the Prague 91st will enter the system and secure the outpost.

# Silent Death

# Scenario 7: "Trial by Combat"

*"Anything?"*

*"Nichts, nothing."*

*"This is getting to be ridiculous. We've been scanning this zone for 3 hours now. If I don't find something to shoot at soon, I'm gonna get antsy."*

*"Well this time, keep your sights off your wingmates—it's bad for morale."*

*"Yeah, Schoen," a third voice came over the radio, "Putting a torp-lock on your commanding officer isn't exactly what I'd call a brilliant career move."*

*"Yeah? Well, I can blast the bad guys just as well without those extra stripes on my sleeve."*

*"Hey, Schoen?" Kazmer returned to the conversation. "What makes you think we're the good guys?"*

*"Cuz the good guys always win."*

*"Schoen, I hate to tell you this, but I think you've been watching the kidsnet instead of the news net."*

*"Um, guys?" A new voice broke into the conversation.*

*"Yeah, kid?"*

*"I hate to interrupt your intellectual discussion, but I seem to have found a squad of fighters in desperate need of being blasted into tiny pieces."*

*"Hot damn! Look out boys, here come the good guys!"*

## Battle

**Date:** AL 9:167

**Location:** The outer reaches of the Ares system

**Situation:** The pirates of "Devil's Luck" have stolen a valuable piece of experimental equipment from one of the science stations in the outer reaches of the Ares system. The Areans won't reveal the nature of the equipment, but are adamant that it be returned. Until the arrival of the Sunrunners, the pirates had been hiding within the system. As the Sunrunners approach the suspected hiding place, the pirates emerge and attempt to flee.

## Forces

### Squadron 3: Windclaw North
### (TPV: 375)

**Commanding officer:** Gregor Radekt (Windjammer)

Set up at edge 4.

| | |
|---|---|
| Windjammer A— | Pilot (Plt 8, Gnr 10, Lck 7) |
| Windjammer B— | Pilot (Plt 7, Gnr 4, Lck 1) |
| Windjammer C— | Pilot (Plt 6, Gnr 5, Lck 1) |
| Wavecutter A— | Pilot (Plt 8, Gnr 5, Lck 1) |
| Wavecutter B— | Pilot (Plt 7, Gnr 4, Lck 1) |
| Dart A— | Pilot (Plt 8, Gnr 5, Lck 1) |
| Dart B— | Pilot (Plt 6, Gnr 4, Lck 1) |
| Salamander A— | Pilot (Plt 8, Gnr 4, Lck 1) |
| | Gunner A (Gnr 6) |
| Salamander B— | Pilot (Plt 7, Gnr 5, Lck 1) |
| | Gunner A (Gnr 7) |

### Devil's Luck, Squad 1 (TPV: 436)

Set up in area E.

| | |
|---|---|
| Night Hawk A— | Pilot (Plt 7, Gnr 6) |
| Night Hawk B— | Pilot (Plt 6, Gnr 5) |
| Night Hawk C— | Pilot (Plt 6, Gnr 5) |
| Night Hawk D— | Pilot (Plt 5, Gnr 4) |
| Thunderbird A— | Pilot (Plt 6, Gnr 8) |
| Thunderbird B— | Pilot (Plt 7, Gnr 4) |
| Thunderbird C— | Pilot (Plt 6, Gnr 5) |
| Thunderbird D— | Pilot (Plt 5, Gnr 4) |
| Teal Hawk A— | Pilot (Plt 7, Gnr 9/Gnr *) |

Arrive on turn 5 at edge 4

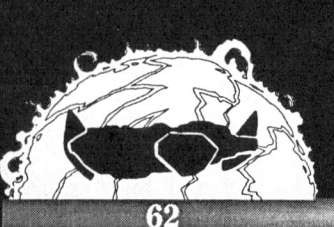

### Squadron 3: Windclaw, South
### (TPV: 386)

| | |
|---|---|
| Windjammer A— | Pilot (Plt 7, Gnr 9, Lck 5) |
| Windjammer B— | Pilot (Plt 8, Gnr 4, Lck 1) |
| Windjammer C— | Pilot (Plt 7, Gnr 5, Lck 1) |
| Wavecutter A— | Pilot (Plt 8, Gnr 4, Lck 1) |
| Wavecutter B— | Pilot (Plt 6, Gnr 6, Lck 1) |
| Havok A— | Pilot (Plt 6, Gnr 5, Lck 1) |
| | Gunner A (Gnr 7) |
| Havok B— | Pilot (Plt 7, Gnr 5, Lck 1) |
| | Gunner A (Gnr 6) |
| Blizzard A— | Pilot (Plt 8, Gnr 4, Lck 1) |
| Blizzard B— | Pilot (Plt 7, Gnr 5, Lck 1) |

Arrive on turn 6 at edge 2

### Devil's Luck, Squad 2, (TPV: 376)

| | |
|---|---|
| Night Hawk A— | Pilot (Plt 7, Gnr 5) |
| Night Hawk B— | Pilot (Plt 6, Gnr 6) |
| Night Hawk C— | Pilot (Plt 5, Gnr 5) |
| Night Hawk D— | Pilot (Plt 6, Gnr 5) |
| Thunderbird A— | Pilot (Plt 6, Gnr 8) |
| Thunderbird B— | Pilot (Plt 7, Gnr 4) |
| Thunderbird C— | Pilot (Plt 6, Gnr 6) |
| Thunderbird D— | Pilot (Plt 5, Gnr 3) |

## Special Rules

1) The pirates' Teal Hawk is carrying the stolen equipment. It should be specially marked. To make room for the stolen item, gunner B has been left behind. All weapons normally under gunner B's control are defunct for this scenario.

2) The goal of this mission is to retrieve the stolen item. If the ship carrying the item is destroyed, the battle is automatically lost.

3) Pirate ships may only leave the playing surface through edge 2. If they leave through edge 2, they reach safety. If they leave the playing surface by any other edge, they are considered destroyed.

4) If the ship carrying the item makes it off the playing surface through edge 2, the battle is lost.

5) The Sunrunners must capture the ship with the item and tow it off the playing surface through edge 4. The Salamanders have tow hooks for this purpose. Once the Teal Hawk has been reduced to a drive of 0, any of the Sunrunner ships equiped with tow hooks can attach to it. This is accomplished by manuevering in front of the Teal Hawk, so that the rear of the Sunrunner ship is facing the front of the Teal Hawk. At this point, the tow hook may immediately and automatically be attached (during the Movement Phase).

## Victory Conditions

The battle is won if the Sunrunners successfully capture the Teal Hawk containing the stolen property and tow it back to Ares (off edge 4). Sunrunners gain a partial victory if all pirates destroyed. All other outcomes are considered a failure.

## A Constitution of Stone

While in the skies above a planet or in the depths of space, the Sunrunners are known for their skill and ferocity in battle. On the planets' surfaces, however, they have gained a reputation for another talent: a taste and tolerance for alcohol unmatched in Terran space. Men and women alike drink the strongest of ale by the liter remain unaffected. While the Sunrunners have spun many tales to explain their prowess, the simple truth is that it comes from long years of practice.

# Scenario 8: "Outlaws"

"Commander, they are a thorn in our sides." The Rattanni ambassador sat easily in his thick high-backed chair. Across from him sat Commander Gregor Radekt, his worn flight suit out of place in the plush office.

"Why not just take them out yourselves? You have the fire power and the forces to do so."

"It would be...politically inadvisable to take direct action at this time. We are, however, in a position to offer the task to you—at your standard fee, of course."

"Of course." Gregor resisted squirming in his seat. Politicians had always made him nervous. He felt they were the result of a bad genetic experiment and should be destroyed as soon as possible. So far, he hadn't been able to find a way that would work. "I'll give you two flights of my own squadron. We'll begin tomorrow. Have all your information sent to my room within the hour." Gregor got up from his seat and headed to the door, only to stop and turn before stepping through it. "And, Ambassador? Those thoughts you're thinking about how to get out of paying us—I'd forget about them right now. It's been a long time since I've had a chance to blast a politician, and I'm starting to think I may need the practice."

## Battle 1

**Date:** AL 9:204
**Location:** Asteroid belt of the Rattanni system
**Situation:** The Sunrunners enter the asteroid field and are immediately attacked from both flanks by a small force of the RPLF.

## Forces

### Sunrunners: Windclaw, North (TPV: 375)

Set up at edge 4 facing direction 1 (Map #1).

| | |
|---|---|
| Windjammer A— | Pilot (Plt 8, Gnr 10, Lck 7) |
| Windjammer B— | Pilot (Plt 7, Gnr 4, Lck 1) |
| Windjammer C— | Pilot (Plt 6, Gnr 5, Lck 1) |
| Wavecutter A— | Pilot (Plt 8, Gnr 5, Lck 1) |
| Wavecutter B— | Pilot (Plt 7, Gnr 4, Lck 1) |
| Dart A— | Pilot (Plt 8, Gnr 5, Lck 1) |
| Dart B— | Pilot (Plt 6, Gnr 4, Lck 1) |
| Salamander A— | Pilot (Plt 8, Gnr 4, Lck 1) |
| | Gunner A (Gnr 6) |
| Salamander B— | Pilot (Plt 7, Gnr 5, Lck 1) |
| | Gunner A (Gnr 7) |

### RPLF: Squad 1 (TPV: 375)

Set up ½ in area A facing direction 3, ½ in area D facing direction 5 (Map #1).

| | |
|---|---|
| Talon A— | Pilot (Plt 6, Gnr 2, Lck 8) |
| Talon B— | Pilot (Plt 5, Gnr 8, Lck 5) |
| Talon C— | Pilot (Plt 4, Gnr 6, Lck 1) |
| Talon D— | Pilot (Plt 4, Gnr 5, Lck 1) |
| Spirit Rider A— | Pilot (Plt 6, Gnr 7, Lck 5) |
| Spirit Rider B— | Pilot (Plt 6, Gnr 5, Lck 4) |
| Spirit Rider C— | Pilot (Plt 5, Gnr 8, Lck 3) |
| Spirit Rider D— | Pilot (Plt 5, Gnr 6, Lck 3) |
| Spirit Rider E— | Pilot (Plt 4, Gnr 5, Lck 1) |
| Spirit Rider F— | Pilot (Plt 1, Gnr 4, Lck 7) |

## Special Rules

1) Ships of the RPLF may flee the battle by exiting the playing field through edge 2 of area B only. Any ship exiting by any other area is considered destroyed but unsalvageable.

2) Before play starts, randomly spread 20 asteroids across the playing field. Try to spread them out to use the entire playing surface.

## Victory Conditions

The battle continues until all the RPLF ships are destroyed or have fled, or all Sunrunner ships are destroyed. The remaining force is the victor.

# Battle 2

**Date:** AL 9:206

**Location:** The asteroid field of the Rattanni system.

**Situation:** A second flight of Sunrunners enters the asteroid field in search of an RPLF squad. The RPLF squad is waiting for them as they enter.

## Forces

### Sunrunners: Windclaw, West (TPV: 365)

| | |
|---|---|
| Wavecutter A— | Pilot (Plt 8, Gnr 4, Lck 7) |
| Wavecutter B— | Pilot (Plt 7, Gnr 6, Lck 1) |
| Blizzard A— | Pilot (Plt 8, Gnr 5, Lck 1) |
| Blizzard B— | Pilot (Plt 8, Gnr 4, Lck 1) |
| Blizzard C— | Pilot (Plt 7, Gnr 5, Lck 1) |
| Teal Hawk A— | Pilot (Plt 9, Gnr 6, Lck 1) |
| | Gunner A (Gnr 7) |
| Teal Hawk B— | Pilot (Plt 8, Gnr 3, Lck 1) |
| | Gunner A (Gnr 6) |
| Teal Hawk C— | Pilot (Plt 7, Gnr 2, Lck 1) |
| | Gunner A (Gnr 5) |

### RPLF: Squad 2, (TPV: 369)

| | |
|---|---|
| Talon A— | Pilot (Plt 7, Gnr 10, Lck 7) |
| Talon B— | Pilot (Plt 5, Gnr 7, Lck 5) |
| Talon C— | Pilot (Plt 4, Gnr 6) |
| Talon D— | Pilot (Plt 4, Gnr 5) |
| Spirit Rider A— | Pilot (Plt 6, Gnr 7, Lck 5) |
| Spirit Rider B— | Pilot (Plt 6, Gnr 5, Lck 4) |
| Spirit Rider C— | Pilot (Plt 5, Gnr 7) |
| Spirit Rider D— | Pilot (Plt 5, Gnr 6) |
| Spirit Rider E— | Pilot (Plt 4, Gnr 5) |
| Spirit Rider F— | Pilot (Plt 3, Gnr 1) |

## Special Rules

1) Pick 3 asteroid counters and mark them differently from the rest (e.g., with a piece of tape). These asteroids are high in radioactive materials. They have an effect-range of 5 hexes. Any ship within that range cannot achieve a missile lock or use electronic counter-measures. Also, any torps within that range lose their lock should be removed from play (This means that a ship within the effect-range cannot fire a torp).

2) There are an additional 15 normal asteroids placed randomly on the map.

3) If, by chance, the 3 special asteroids end up close enough together that an area of the playing surface is within the effect-ranges of ALL 3 asteroids, that area becomes a "dead zone." Any ships entering that area are immediately disabled and are "dead in the water," and any crew members on those ships die. The dead ships are salvageable if they can be removed from the dead zone.

## Victory Conditions

The battle continues until all ships of one side are destroyed or disabled. The remaining force is the victor.

# Scenario 9: "Rip Tide"

In addition to the normal host of warriors, support crews, and other personnel common to a carrier, the Sunrunner carriers have one additional crew: the cats. The cats roam freely about the ship's passageways and access gangways hunting the various vermin that get aboard with various food shipments or other incoming stock. A normal carrier will support a host of 50-100 cats at any one time. The cats live off of the vermin they catch, as well as the various scraps and treats that the crew regularly give them.

After several generations onboard the carriers, the feline warriors are excellently adapted to the conditions. They are able to move perfectly in a wide variety of gravities, including zero-g conditions. They have learned the "flora" of the jungle of cabling and piping that makes up a vast majority of

*It is the beginning of the holy days on Vian. For two weeks the entire population sets aside its work and joins in the sometimes quiet, sometimes wild celebrations recounting the cycles of life. The other worlds of Terran space know very little about the Vian monks. They know even less about their religion or calendar. This year, however, a small band of pirates has done their homework and are expecting easy pickings. There's just one catch...*

## Battle

**Date:** AL 9:224
**Location:** Just outside the orbit of Vian
**Situation:** The Viani have received information that a pirate raid is scheduled during one of their religious feasts. Being unable to fight during a holy day, they have hired the Sunrunners to face the pirates in their place. At the beginning of the battle, the Sunrunners slip out from behind one of the moons of Vian V to confront the unsuspecting pirates.

## Forces

### Sunrunners: God's Frost, East (TPV: 1077)

Set up in area H.

| | |
|---|---|
| Avenger A— | Pilot (Plt 8, Gnr 7, Lck 4) |
| | Gunner A (Gnr 7) |
| Pharsii II A— | Pilot (Plt 6, Gnr 6, Lck 3) |
| | Gunner A (Gnr 8) |
| | Gunner B (Gnr 7) |
| Pharsii II B— | Pilot (Plt 5, Gnr 6, Lck 3) |
| | Gunner A (Gnr 7) |
| | Gunner B (Gnr 6) |
| Spider A— | Pilot (Plt 7, Gnr 6, Lck 3) |
| | Gunner A (Gnr 8) |
| | Gunner B (Gnr 7) |
| Spider B— | Pilot (Plt 6, Gnr 6, Lck 3) |
| | Gunner A (Gnr 7) |
| | Gunner B (Gnr 7) |
| Havok A— | Pilot (Plt 6, Gnr 6, Lck 3) |
| | Gunner A (Gnr 6) |
| Catastrophe A— | Pilot (Plt 7, Gnr 5, Lck 3) |
| | Gunner A (Gnr 7) |
| | Gunner B (Gnr 7) |
| | Gunner C (Gnr 6) |
| Sorenson III A— | Pilot (Plt 6, Gnr 5, Lck 3) |
| | Gunner A (Gnr 7) |

### Pirates: Wildcats, Pirate force (TPV: 1060)

Set up in area B.

| | |
|---|---|
| Salamander A— | Pilot (Plt 7, Gnr 7, Lck 3) |
| | Gunner A (Gnr 6) |
| Salamander B— | Pilot (Plt 7, Gnr 6) |
| | Gunner A (Gnr 5) |
| Salamander C— | Pilot (Plt 6, Gnr 5) |
| | Gunner A (Gnr 6) |
| Salamander D— | Pilot (Plt 4, Gnr 6) |
| | Gunner A (Gnr 5) |
| Teal Hawk A— | Pilot (Plt 7, Gnr 5) |
| | Gunner A (Gnr 8) |
| Teal Hawk B— | Pilot (Plt 6, Gnr 4) |
| | Gunner A (Gnr 5) |
| Teal Hawk C— | Pilot (Plt 6, Gnr 1) |
| | Gunner A (Gnr 7) |
| Teal Hawk D— | Pilot (Plt 5, Gnr 1) |
| | Gunner A (Gnr 5) |
| Hell Bender A— | Pilot (Plt 6, Gnr 8) |
| Hell Bender B— | Pilot (Plt 6, Gnr 7) |
| Hell Bender C— | Pilot (Plt 5, Gnr 5) |
| Hell Bender D— | Pilot (Plt 1, Gnr 3) |
| Sorenson III A— | Pilot (Plt 6, Gnr 7) |
| | Gunner A (Gnr 6) |
| Sorenson III B— | Pilot (Plt 5, Gnr 7) |
| | Gunner A (Gnr 5) |
| Sorenson III B— | Pilot (Plt 4, Gnr 2) |
| | Gunner A (Gnr 6) |
| Sorenson III B— | Pilot (Plt 1, Gnr 3) |
| | Gunner A (Gnr 3) |

## Special Rules

**1)** If the pirate force falls below 8 ships, they may retreat back through edge 2.

## Victory Conditions

The battle lasts until the Sunrunners are all destroyed or disabled or the pirates are all destroyed or disabled or retreat. The remaining force is the victor.

# Scenario 10: "THE WALL"

*"High above me in orbit, the battles have already begun. The might of the Bokchito collective is again flexing its muscles against its smaller neighbors. This time, it's against the small agricultural planet known as Homestead. The Homesteaders are farmers, merchants and simple craftsman. Yet despite all the odds, they have withstood the assaults of some of the most powerful nations in the frontier. This time, however, the Homesteaders have called in help. The outlaw Sunrunners are holding position above the planet at this very moment, waiting to face the forces of Bokchito's 29th planetary assault wing—more commonly known as the Iron Rain. And that's the question running through the minds of those around me. Will the rain of the clouds gathering at the horizon be the cool water of life or the shrieking steel of death?" Kathleen Baca, UniNet News, Homestead.*

## Battle 1

**Date:** AL 9:265
**Location:** Within the orbit of KZ-24N9, IV
**Situation:** Homestead is again under attack by Bokchi forces. The Homesteaders have hired the Sunrunners as a defensive force.

## Forces:

### Sunrunner Squadron 2: Stormbringer South (TPV: 1265)

Set up along edge 4.

| | |
|---|---|
| Glaive A— | Pilot (Plt 8, Gnr 9, Lck 4) |
| | Gunner A (Gnr 8) |
| Catastrophe A— | Pilot (Plt 8, Gnr 8, Lck 3) |
| | Gunner A (Gnr 8) |
| | Gunner B (Gnr 7) |
| | Gunner C (Gnr 6) |
| Catastrophe B— | Pilot (Plt 7, Gnr 7, Lck3) |
| | Gunner A (Gnr 8) |
| | Gunner B (Gnr 7) |
| | Gunner C (Gnr 5) |
| Catastrophe C— | Pilot (Plt 6, Gnr 8, Lck3) |
| | Gunner A (Gnr 7) |
| | Gunner B (Gnr 6) |
| | Gunner C (Gnr 6) |
| Pharsii II A— | Pilot (Plt 8, Gnr 8, Lck 2) |
| | Gunner A (Gnr 7) |
| | Gunner B (Gnr 6) |
| Pharsii II B— | Pilot (Plt 7, Gnr 7, Lck 2) |
| | Gunner A (Gnr 7) |
| | Gunner B (Gnr 6) |
| Pharsii II C— | Pilot (Plt 6, Gnr 8, Lck 2) |
| | Gunner A (Gnr 6) |
| | Gunner B (Gnr 5) |
| Hell Bender A— | Pilot (Plt 8, Gnr 7, Lck 2) |
| Hell Bender B— | Pilot (Plt 7, Gnr 7, Lck 2) |
| Hell Bender C— | Pilot (Plt 7, Gnr 6, Lck 2) |

### Squad 1 Bokchito: Iron Rain, Squad 2 (TPV: 1120)

Set up in area B and C.

| | |
|---|---|
| Betafortress Alpha A— | Pilot (Plt 7, Gnr 8) |
| | Gunner A (Gnr 6) |
| | Gunner B (Gnr 6) |
| | Gunner C (Gnr 6) |
| | Gunner D (Gnr 6) |
| | Gunner E (Gnr 6) |
| Betafortress Alpha B— | Pilot (Plt 6, Gnr 7) |
| | Gunner A (Gnr 5) |
| | Gunner B (Gnr 5) |
| | Gunner C (Gnr 5) |
| | Gunner D (Gnr 5) |
| | Gunner E (Gnr 6) |
| Sorenson III A— | Pilot (Plt 6, Gnr 8) |
| | Gunner A (Gnr 6) |
| Sorenson III B— | Pilot (Plt 5, Gnr 6) |
| | Gunner A (Gnr 5) |
| Sorenson III B— | Pilot (Plt 5, Gnr 5) |
| | Gunner A (Gnr 6) |
| Sorenson III B— | Pilot (Plt 3, Gnr 5) |
| | Gunner A (Gnr 4) |
| Revenge A— | Pilot (Plt 6, Gnr 1) |
| | Gunner A (Gnr 6) |
| Revenge B— | Pilot (Plt 5, Gnr 1) |
| | Gunner A (Gnr 5) |

## Special Rules

**1)** Bokchi forces may exit the playing surface through edge 4 or edge 2. Those that exit by edge two are considered to have fled and cannot be considered in reinforcements in Battle 2. Those exiting through edge 4 are allowed as reinforcements in Battle 2.

the ships' systems, and know what items to avoid approaching. They are also quite good at finding pinhole leaks in the hull or other systems. Whenever a tech sees a cat hissing at a blank wall, a repair kit is brought out immediately, and the leak searched for.

Over the years, the Sunrunners have made a habit of giving gifts of kittens to commanders of allied forces. This is yet another way in which they have formed friendships that extend beyond the simple business dealings. These friendships are the connections that eventually lead to important and profitable dealings later on.

## Victory Conditions

The battle continues until one side no longer has any functional ships on the playing surface. Sunrunners claims a victory only if less than 8 Bokchi ships survive to move on to Homestead (including those that passed through edge 4 during the battle).

# Battle 2

**Date:** AL 9:266

**Location:** Just outside the orbit of Homestead

**Situation:** The Sunrunners prepare to battle the second half of the Bokchi assault.

## Forces

### Sunrunners: Stormbringer, West (TPV: 911)

Set up along edge 4.

| | |
|---|---|
| Drakar A— | Pilot (Plt 8, Gnr 8, Lck3) |
| | Gunner A (Gnr 8) |
| | Gunner B (Gnr 7) |
| | Gunner C (Gnr 6) |
| | Gunner D (Gnr 6) |
| Hell Bender A— | Pilot (Plt 8, Gnr 7, Lck 2) |
| Hell Bender B— | Pilot (Plt 7, Gnr 7, Lck 2) |
| Glaive A— | Pilot (Plt 8, Gnr 9, Lck 2) |
| | Gunner A (Gnr 7) |
| Glaive B— | Pilot (Plt 7, Gnr 8, Lck 2) |
| | Gunner A (Gnr 8) |
| Sentry A— | Pilot (Plt 8, Gnr 7, Lck 2) |
| | Gunner A (Gnr 8) |
| | Gunner B (Gnr 7) |
| Sentry B— | Pilot (Plt 7, Gnr 7, Lck 2) |
| | Gunner A (Gnr 7) |
| | Gunner B (Gnr 8) |
| Sentry C— | Pilot (Plt 6, Gnr 5, Lck 2) |
| | Gunner A (Gnr 5) |
| | Gunner B (Gnr 6) |

### Bokchito: Iron Rain, Squad (TPV: 11241)

Set up along edge 2.

| | |
|---|---|
| Betafortress Beta A— | Pilot (Plt 8, Gnr 7) |
| | Gunner A (Gnr 6) |
| | Gunner B (Gnr 5) |
| | Gunner C (Gnr 7) |
| | Gunner D (Gnr 6) |
| | Gunner E (Gnr 6) |
| Betafortress Beta B— | Pilot (Plt 6, Gnr 7) |
| | Gunner A (Gnr 6) |
| | Gunner B (Gnr 5) |
| | Gunner C (Gnr 4) |
| | Gunner D (Gnr 5) |
| | Gunner E (Gnr 6) |
| Sorenson III A— | Pilot (Plt 7, Gnr 7) |
| | Gunner A (Gnr 5) |
| Sorenson III B— | Pilot (Plt 5, Gnr 7) |
| | Gunner A (Gnr 5) |
| Sorenson III C— | Pilot (Plt 5, Gnr 4) |
| | Gunner A (Gnr 7) |
| Sorenson III D— | Pilot (Plt 3, Gnr 5) |
| | Gunner A (Gnr 4) |
| Revenge A— | Pilot (Plt 6, Gnr 1) |
| | Gunner A (Gnr 6) |
| Revenge B— | Pilot (Plt 5, Gnr 1) |
| | Gunner A (Gnr 5) |

## Reinforcements [optional]

• Remains of Iron Rain, Squad 2 from Battle 1

• Remains of Stormbringer, Squad 1 from Battle 1

## Special Rules

1) [optional] After the 5th turn, the remains of the Bokchi squad from Battle 1 may enter through edge 2. After the 7th turn, the remains of the Sunrunner squad from Battle 1 may enter through edge 2.

2) The Bokchi forces may retreat at any time by leaving the playing surface through edge 2. This may be done on a per ship basis or as a force. Any ship which flees may not return.

3) Any Sunrunner ship may retreat by exiting the playing field through edge 4. Any ship which flees may not return.

4) Any ship which leaves the playing surface (except as in rules #2 or #3) is considered to be destroyed. Kill Bonus rules are in effect, but these ships may not be salvaged.

## Victory Conditions

The battle lasts until one side no longer has any fighting ships left on the playing surface. The remaining force is the victor.

# Scenario 11: "Blood Feud"

*"So basically what you're saying is that they're going to pay us to be annoying."*
*"Yep."*
*"I like this job."*

## Battle 1

**Date:** AL 9:282
**Location:** Above Trask in the system KDL-34NX5
**Situation:** The Sunrunners have been hired by Argent to harass the defensive forces Taber has stationed on Trask. The government of Argent is not concerned with capturing the planet yet, only with causing aggravation for the Taber forces stationed there.

## Forces

### Sunrunners: Jacob's Thunder, West flight Taber: Screaming Mimi, Squad 1 West (TPV: 567)

Setup in area H facing direction 6 (Map #1).

| | |
|---|---|
| Sorenson III A— | Pilot (Plt 9, Gnr 7, Lck 4) |
| | Gunner A (Gnr 7) |
| Sorenson III B— | Pilot (Plt 8, Gnr 6, Lck 2) |
| | Gunner A (Gnr 6) |
| Sorenson III C— | Pilot (Plt 7, Gnr 6, Lck 2) |
| | Gunner A (Gnr 6) |
| Sorenson III D— | Pilot (Plt 8, Gnr 5, Lck 2) |
| | Gunner A (Gnr 5) |
| Salamander A— | Pilot (Plt 8, Gnr 7, Lck 2) |
| | Gunner A (Gnr 9) |
| Wavecutter A— | Pilot (Plt 8, Gnr 6, Lck 2) |
| Wavecutter B— | Pilot (Plt 7, Gnr 5, Lck 2) |
| Thunderbird A— | Pilot (Plt 5, Gnr 7, Lck 2) |

### Taber 23rd Defensive Wing (TPV: 866)

Set up in area A facing direction 3 TPV.

| | |
|---|---|
| Sorenson III A— | Pilot (Plt 7, Gnr 5) |
| | Gunner A (Gnr 8) |
| Sorenson III B— | Pilot (Plt 6, Gnr 7) |
| | Gunner A (Gnr 5) |
| Sorenson III C— | Pilot (Plt 6, Gnr 4) |
| | Gunner A (Gnr 7) |
| Sorenson III D— | Pilot (Plt 6, Gnr 5) |
| | Gunner A (Gnr 4) |
| Sorenson III E— | Pilot (Plt 5, Gnr 5) |
| | Gunner A (Gnr 4) |
| Sorenson III F— | Pilot (Plt 4, Gnr 7) |
| | Gunner A (Gnr 5) |
| Sorenson III G— | Pilot (Plt 3, Gnr 4) |
| | Gunner A (Gnr 7) |
| Sorenson III H— | Pilot (Plt 1, Gnr 2) |
| | Gunner A (Gnr 1) |
| Sentry A— | Pilot (Plt 6, Gnr 6) |
| | Gunner A (Gnr 6) |
| | Gunner B (Gnr 5) |
| Sentry B— | Pilot (Plt 6, Gnr 5) |
| | Gunner A (Gnr 5) |
| | Gunner B (Gnr 5) |

## Special Rules

**1)** The Sunrunner ships may leave the playing surface at any time and return to it up to 5 hexes away after three turns.

## Victory Conditions

The battle lasts for 20 turns. The Sunrunners are victorious if there are fewer than 5 ships with over half of their damage track unmarked.

If all Sunrunner ships are off the playing surface for more than 1 full turn, they lose.

# Campaign Creation Guidelines

## Thor's Hammer

Though the Sunrunners are not ones for jewelry or fashion, there is one piece of adornment that is extremely common among them: Thor's Hammer. The ancient amulet, originally a sign of strength, has taken on an additional meaning in the Sunrunner culture. The father of the modern Sunrunners was Tomass "Thor" Bach. Under his leadership, following that of his father Michael, the Sunrunners came to be a power in their own right. It was also his philosophy of warfare that was shaped into the fighting code of the Sunrunners. A major aspect of that philosophy is that the life of one warrior is a sacred thing, yet means nothing if he is unwilling to sacrifice it in the name of his beliefs.

Like his father before him, Tomass died in an heroic—and perhaps arrogant—manner. In

---

For those players wishing to create their own games within the *Silent Death* system, a set of campaign creation rules and guidelines is being written [Check with your local retailer]. While the full campaign system is still forthcoming for the *Silent Death* system, the Second Edition does include a set of rules for creating a Mini-campaign. These rules may be used to create and run a Sunrunner force of your own, keeping in mind the guidelines below when doing so. There are two changes to the Mini-campaign rules as written in the Second Edition in order to fit them to a Sunrunner fleet. 1) Sunrunners get no points if they loose or draw. 2) The Sunrunners DO get points for salvaged ships and for the KILL BONUS as explained in *"SPOILS OF WAR"* on page 19 and ransom as explained on page 20.

### Fleet Organization

A full breakdown of the forces aboard the *Maelstrom*, and a basic breakdown of the forces aboard the *Vulcan* and *Huntress*, are given on page 27. Besides these forces, there are two new carriers, the *Avalanche* and *Ground Zero*, awaiting final fittings before their commission, and three more, the *Firefall, Eclipse*, and *Tempest,* are under various stages of construction. Each of these new carriers will hold a force of four squadrons, as do the current carriers, with a breakdown like the one described on page 27. Each carrier is essentially an independent force, making their own business arrangements, but being ultimately answering to the admiral aboard the *Maelstrom*.

### Component Starcraft

In the new carriers, the initial forces will be made of mostly Coring and Kip-Kanzer fighters, with a few others added to fill certain gaps. As the carriers go about their business, the make-up of the fleet will change, with the addition of captured craft, and the loss of original ones. In creating a fighting force, take into consideration the

---

time the carrier has been out. If it's a short time, the inventory will be between half and all Sunrunner craft, while a force that has been fighting for some time could be half or less Sunrunner ships. A minimum of the craft in any squadron should be of Sunrunner origin.

### Nomenclature

The wing attached to any carrier is named according to the carrier's name. Each carrier—with the exception of two of the originals—is named for some sort of cataclysmic event or destructive force. The wing should take a name reflecting that type of cataclysm [*Maelstrom*: White Wind]. The squadrons beneath that do the same, though often using the name of their commander within it [Jacob's Thunder]. The flights within each squadron are named for the cardinal points of the compass: North, South, East, and West. Commanders are part of North flight. When flying in formation, the flights form a diamond corresponding to the compass points.

When choosing names for their fighting forces, the Sunrunners tend to pick those with mythical or primitive connotations such as forces of nature generally attributed to the anger of the gods.

### The Campaign

As you play these extended games, and take your Sunrunner fleet against opponent after opponent, other factors begin to enter into the games. Keeping track of the ransom and KILL BONUS becomes very important. This is the only way for you to replenish the ships in your fleet. It's also a way for you to change the make up of your fleet and create a fleet that better fits your needs. Also, increasing the skill of your pilots and gunners is possible. This means that the ships are not just cannon fodder, but are fighters with skilled crews. Loosing a ship or its crew has an effect on the battles that will come after.

# Starcraft Inventory and Nomenclenture

## Kip Kanzer KBL-29 "AVENGER"

**Crew:** 2
**Maneuvering Thrust:** 0.138 Km/s/s
**Mass:** 620 tons
**Translight Capability:** None
**Armor:** Crysteel
**Atmospheric Capability:** None
**Armaments:**  2x Meld Laser
1x EMP Beam
4x Mk 20 Stinger Torps
10x Mk 10 Venter Torps

The first ship original to the Sunrunners, the AVENGER is a two-person attack craft with heavy armament and medium armor. The speed is somewhat sacrificed in favor of the heavier weapons. One of the main advantages of the AVENGER is that it is designed to use parts from several other ships as replacements, and can be easily fitted with any number of weapons. So far, the Sunrunners are the only organization to use the AVENGER. They do, however, hope to sell some of these ships to colonies and smaller governments.

The AVENGER is suited for attacking larger ships and gunboats. It can hold it's own in the firepower area, while still having the ability to get away from the slower gunboats. It works well as the backbone to a force of smaller craft.

## Coring KV-105 "WAVECUTTER"

**Crew:** 1
**Maneuvering Thrust:** 0.187 Km/s/s
**Mass:** 210 tons
**Translight Capability:** None
**Armor:** Crysteel
**Atmospheric Capability:** Full
**Armaments:**  1x EMP Ray
2x Pulse Laser

The Coring fighters were the primary craft of Barat-Tuul, the now-destroyed homeworld of the Sunrunners. The experimental Coring craft were gaining popularity, but further development was cut short by the invasion of the Night Brood. In recent years, production of the WAVECUTTER and other Coring craft has been reinitiated by the Sunrunners and others who have purchased the designs. The first of the Coring craft to reach mass production, the WAVECUTTER is a SPAC with exceptional speed and maneuverability, making it quite hard to hit. The very light armor, however, doesn't give much protection once it is hit.

The WAVECUTTER is hit-and-run type of fighter craft. Like the DART, SPIRIT RIDER, and other small ships, it best utilizes it's strengths by attacking quickly and then getting out of range until another chance to attack arises. Because of their speed, the WAVECUTTER is also a good ship to take the point, and occupy the enemy until the slower ships can arrive.

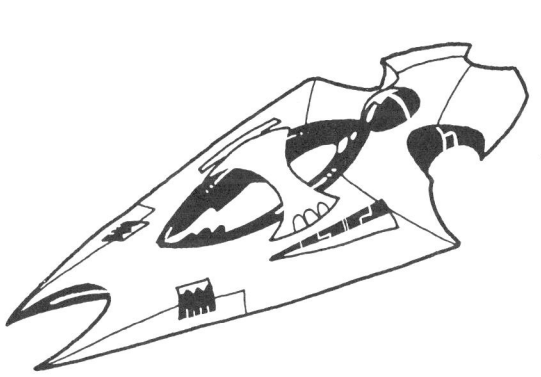

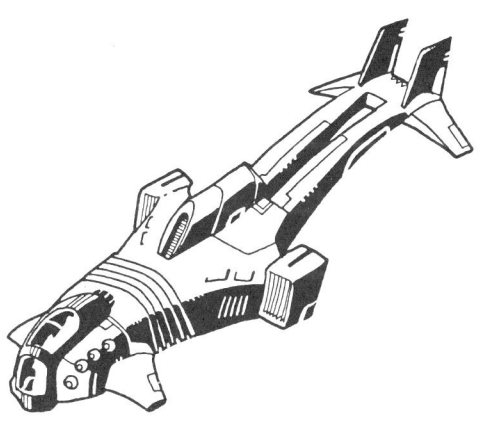

a battle which pitted the Sunrunners against a Brood swarm, the Sunrunners were facing a very real possibility of defeat.

The Brood star fighters were acting as the main fighter force, engaging the enemy one-on-one, while behind their protective force, sat a heavily armed battle pod. Its payload of warheads sat patiently in the belly of the beast, anxiously awaiting the planetary bombardment that was their goal. Unlike other Brood carriers ships before it, this carrier bristled with weaponry. Either way, it was the massive guns of the battle pod that were decimating the smaller fighter craft of Sunrunner forces preventing them from attaining the destructive victory they sought.

A message broadcast across the fighter band—it's origin: Admiral Tomass Bach. "Any 'Runner to leave this space with breath to tell of defeat, shall face my wrath at the Bridge—and that of Odin as well." *Odin?*

*The mythic god? Or the dead admiral, Tomass' father? The questions flashed across several minds? On what ship's bridge will he be that he might stand by either?* They soon found their answer.

His gunner unconscious, his weaponry taken out, Tomass made a desperation play to protect the wings under his command. He knew his Avenger *Mjolnir* was in no condition to take on the fighter craft of the enemy. Giving the engine all the power he could, he dove straight through the attacking fighters toward the battleship. Angling his approach so as to come at the rear-quadrant of the massive ship, he punched is engines into an over-load state and drove straight into the engine ports of the hulk, arming the 3 torps still onboard as he did so.

A savage explosion ripped through the ship as the power source encountered the ramming ship and its

## Coring HaV-205 "HAVOK"

**Crew:** 2
**Maneuvering Thrust:** 0.150 Km/s/s
**Mass:** 400 tons
**Translight Capability:** None
**Armor:** Crysteel
**Atmospheric Capability:** Full
**Armaments:**  2x Meld Laser
1x EMP Beam
3x Pulse Lasers
4x Mk 10 Stinger Torps

The HaV-205 HAVOK is the second generation of Coring craft. It has an additional gunner. Again, armor is sacrificed for speed and maneuverability.

The HAVOK is an all-around fighter. While is doesn't have any particular feature which sets it apart, it is able to work effectively in any number of situations. The lower-end armor does act as a drawback when involved in extended battles.

## Coring Db-395 "CATASTROPHE"

**Crew:** 4
**Maneuvering Thrust:** 0.099 Km/s/s
**Mass:** 1050 tons
**Translight Capability:** None
**Armor:** Crystanium
**Atmospheric Capability:**
Severely limited w/ belt
**Armaments:**  6x Mk 20 Stinger Torps
10x Mk 10 Venter Torps
2x EMP Beam
2x EMP Rays
1x Missile Launcher
(mag:20)
3x Pulse Lasrs
1x Turbo Laser
4x Meld Laser

Seeing the need for a larger, more heavily armed ship, Coring developed the CATASTROPHE [pronounced: CAT-ah-strof]. The size of the CATASTROPHE allows it to carry a payload of both missiles and torpedoes, as well as electronic counter measures. The CATASTROPHE has one additional feature: the ability of any of the gunners to take control of another gunner's (or the pilot's) gunning position from their own station. The pilots may only fire from their own position.

The CATASTROPHE is the heavy armament of the Sunrunners, and is used as such. Like any other gunboat, it's main purpose is to wade into the middle of the fight and start meting out the punishment. In this respect, the CATASTROPHE does very well. In just about any other situation, though, it is too slow to be of much use. One or two of these, with a host of smaller ships, are able to last for a fair amount of time in a battle.

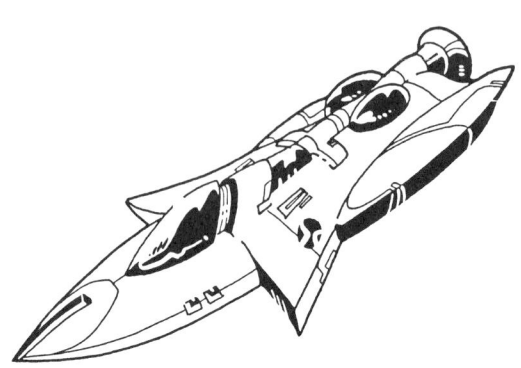

## Inmar 026 "WINDJAMMER"

**Crew:** 1
**Maneuvering Thrust:** 0.177 Km/s/s
**Mass:** 105 tons
**Translight Capability:** None
**Armor:** Crysteel w/ belt
**Atmospheric Capability:** Full
**Armaments:** 5x Pulse Laser

Inmar's WINDJAMMER is an SPAC designed in response to the PIT VIPER. The WINDJAMMER is also better designed for atmospheric flight, and handles exceptionally well even in difficult atmospheric conditions. This makes it an excellent craft for planets which can't afford orbital stations. The WINDJAMMER is otherwise about equally matched with the PIT VIPER, carrying a slightly higher price tag due to the additional lasers. It is, however, freely marketed, and available to anyone with the cash.

The WINDJAMMER is another of the small hit-and-run type fighters that are easy to use and easy to replace. They work best against ships their own size or slightly larger, though have the potential to do some damage against the big ships. Their inability to take much damage makes them a poor choice for extended battles.

## Inmar 049 "SPIDER"

**Crew:** 3
**Maneuvering Thrust:** 0.083 Km/s/s
**Mass:** 1100 tons
**Translight Capability:** 7 light-years/day
**Armor:** Crystanium w/ belt
**Atmospheric Capability:** None
**Armaments:**
| | |
|---|---|
| 10x Mk 10 Stinger Torps |
| 6x Mk 20 Venter Torps |
| 1x Tractor beam |
| 1x Ion Ram |
| 1x Turbo Lasers |
| 2x Meld Lasers |
| 1x Missile Launcher |
| (Mag 20) |

The SPIDER is a three-person craft designed to fight alongside the WINDJAMMER. Two or three SPIDERs within a flight of WINDJAMMERs fill out the flight and add the heavy fire power to back up the smaller craft. The armament of the SPIDER is mainly torpedoes, but is supplemented by two 360° Meld lasers on a turret above and a Ion ram below. The SPIDER is slow, but strong, and only a few are needed give backbone to a fighting force.

The SPIDER is a ship designed for battles which need a large amount of firepower, but aren't expected to last for very long. The SPIDER's battery of torps is impressive, but once it is depleted, the ship has little in cannons for a ship of this size. It achieves its best results in conjunction with a host of small or medium-sized ships to protect it while it moves in to a selected target. This works well when moving against a space-station or satellite.

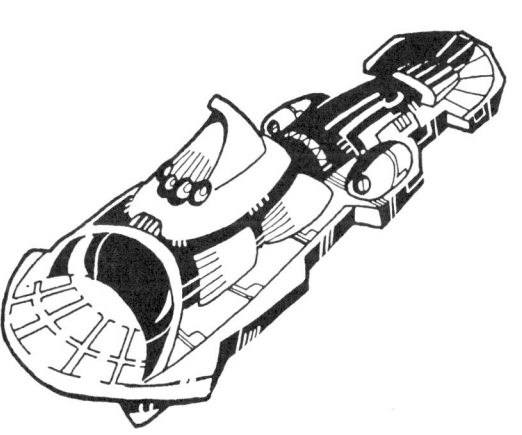

payload. The rear quarter of the battle pod virtually vaporized; the remainder damaged beyond hope. Without it's significant armament to give power to the outnumbered swarm, the Sunrunners slowly managed to destroy the swarm to the very last ship. Only 9 ships returned from the battle. Badly damaged, many of their crews dead and dying, they told the story of the victory and the devastation inflicted by Mjolnir. It was only after their return, that the last message from the Admiral became clear. He would stand beside his father—Thor and Odin, shoulder to shoulder—at the Bridge of Jdalerbru; the sole passage into the mythical land of the dead.

Since that battle, the Sunrunners have paid tribute to their fallen leader in two ways, one small yet significant, the other grand and powerful. Virtually all warriors—as well as many other among the population—wear a silver amulet of Thor's hammer; it's sharp,

clean edges often worn round, scratched and nicked with the evidence of long wear. It is a symbol of their commitment to their ultimate cause and a statement of what they are willing to sacrifice to achieve it. Tomass's greatest sacrifice was not that he gave his life to the battle—any warrior would do no less—it was that he sacrificed the life of his gunner; Lieutenant Valor Katerin Bach—his eldest daughter.

After the end of the Second Hatchling War (see Night Brood: Armageddon) those left in power organized the creation of special wings of fighter craft designed solely for the purpose of combating the Brood (see Night Watch). Though not officially sanctioned, the Sunrunners have their own wing of Night Watch fighters: Thor's Hammer. The best of the best, these warriors are dedicated to the ultimate extermination of the Brood menace from Terran space.

# OPTIONAL RULES

## Alternative Control Gunnery Positions

The Coring Db-395 "CATASTROPHE" has the unusual feature of alternate control gunnery positions. This means that any one of the three gunners may take control of any of the four gunnery positions (the fourth being the pilot's) and fire them from his own controls. The pilot may only fire from his own position.

Any change of gunnery positions must be announced at the beginning of the turn before the launching of missiles and/or torps. The gunner announces which position he will be moving to, and which weapon will be taken control of. If there is more than one functional weapon at that position, both may be used at the same time, one by each gunner. The gunner must remain at the new position for the full turn, and then may return to his own on the next or remain at the new position. The gunner is considered to stay at the new position unless announced that he is moving again. During any turn in which a gunner changes position, that gunner may only fire cannon weapons.

The sequence is as follows:
Announcement of gunnery position change
Missile/torp launch (excluding moving gunner)
Torp results
Cannon fire (including moved gunner)
Missile results

## Minimal Tight turns

To perform a tight turn the ship must have at least the minimum necessary movement points to perform the maneuver. Before rolling the player must specify which direction the ship is turning. (right or left) If the turn ends up costing more movement points than the ship has left this phase, the craft turns one hex facing in the direction of the turn.

# APPENDIX A

## Worlds of the Frontier

### Barat-Tuul

**System**: Barat
**World**: Barat-Tuul
**Class**: Planet
**Natural Satellites:** None
**State**: Barat Free State
**Status**: System capitol
**Autonomy**: High
**Evironment**: Industrialized
**Habitat**: Normal
**Gravity**: 1.3
**Atmosphere**: Normal
**% H$_2$O**: 63
**Mean Temp** — 00 lat: s 75 / w 50
450 lat: s 60 / w 20
**Diameter**: 98,200 km
**Axial Tilt**: 180
**Day**: 29.1 hrs
**Year**: 402.1 days
**Danger**: None
**Race**: Barat
**Population**: 4 billion
**Social Adaptations**: Proud, warrior-like, disregard for death
**Trade**: Military fighter craft and ordnance
**Government**: Limited monarchy

**Notes**: The information above is for Barat at its height. It is now a barren system overrun by Grubs.

### Bethany

**System**: Beta 795
**World**: Bethany
**Class**: Planet
**Natural Satellites**: 1, Dio
**State**: N/Ap
**Status**: Independent
**Autonomy**: Full
**Evironment**: Lush vegetation
**Habitat**: Normal
**Gravity**: 0.9
**Atmosphere**: Normal
**% H$_2$O**: 57
**Mean Temp** — 00 lat: s 100 / w 80
450 lat: s 90 / w 50
**Diameter**: 10,400 km
**Axial Tilt**: 120
**Day**: 37.4 hours
**Year**: 627.8 days
**Danger**: Hostile Vegetation
**Race**: Bethan
**Population**: 176 million
**Social Adaptations**: Superiority of females
**Trade**: Organic compounds, drugs, medicines.
**Government**: Matriarchy

**Notes**: When the Grubs came to the far Frontier planet of Bethany, the poulation was not ready to handle the attack. While they had a sizable military fleet on lease from the Empire, the men manning the ships were inexperienced in their use. The first wave of Grubs essentially wiped out the defensive force. but without claiming the planet. In the second wave, virtually every able-bodied man took to the air, and through sheer luck repelled the Grubs, but at a cost of over 90 percent of the men. Breaking from the highly gender-restrictive tradition, the third wave was comprised almost entirely of women. Through pure determination and guts, they did what the men could not: they drove the Grubs back, inflicting heavy casualties on them in the process. After that, the Grubs left the planet alone.

In the aftermath, the women set about rebuilding their society. The severe lack of able-bodied men caused several major changes, including a major revision in traditional gender roles. Since that time, Bethany has regained some of it's former strength in the economic arena, producing some of the more important medicines and recreational drugs within Terran space. With the coming of the Prometheans, they have opened a whole new market. They deal with the Primates both directly and indirectly, while spurning the Draconians. Their dealings with the Primates remain of a business nature only, and any political overtures are politely rebuffed.

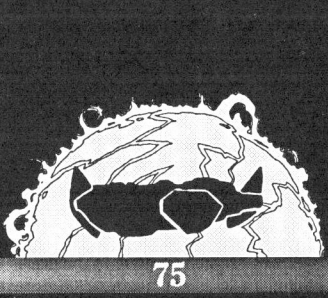

# Silent Death

## Night Visions

"Michael?"

Commander Horst rolled to face his wife. "Yes?"

"Do you think it'll actually happen?"

"What?"

"The Return." She rolled to face him, raising herself up on one elbow. Her left hand absently stroked the thick gray hairs on his chest. "There are days I can barely remember what home looked like."

He sighed deeply and returned to his back. "I've almost come to hope it doesn't happen until after I'm dead. I sit and think about what my parents' home looked like. Or the cabin on Berkynn Lake. It wasn't much, but it was special. I remember taking out the little canoe that Dad had bought for Dolph and I. I used to love to go out alone just as the sun was rising, and paddle slowly past the other cabins and into the little hidden bay on the other side of Lurker's Point."

"I wish I'd been there to see it. Every

76

## Bokchito

**System:** Bokchito
**World:** Bokchito I-VII
**Class:** Planetary system
**Natural Satellites:** None
**State:** Bokchito Collective
**Status:** Independent alliance
**Autonomy:** Full
**Evironment:** Barren rock / Gaseous
**Habitat:** Sealed domes, caverns / Floating airships
**Gravity:** varied
**Atmosphere:** None / Poisonous, caustic
**% H$_2$O:** 0
**Mean Temp** — 00 lat: sN/A / w N/A
    450 lat: s N/A / wN/A
**Diameter:** N/A
**Axial Tilt:** N/A
**Day:** N/A
**Year:** N/A
**Danger:**
**Race:** Bokchi
**Population:** 7.8 billion
**Social Adaptations:** None
**Trade:** Mining
**Government:** Corporate dictatorship

**Notes:** The Bokchito Collective is a system of barren and gaseous worlds surrounding a cool star. The only thing this system has to offer is a vast quantity of heavy metals and rare elements. The miners of the Bokchito Planets have been suppliers for a large portion of the Frontier as well as the fomer Empire. Now that the Empire is ruined and most of the Frontier worlds are too poor to buy for manufacturing purposes, the Bokchi are finding life a little harder. Fortunately, the corporation had stockpiled a large amount of wealth and invested the rest in areas which could survive the death of the Empire. They still lost much with the destruction of the Core, and have taken that setback poorly.

The Bokchi are a hard people, toughened by the harsh conditions under which they have lived. When the Grubs came, the Bokchi quickly converted their mining technologies to war technologies, and stopped the Grubs cold. Not a single landing of a Grub ship upon a Bokchi world occured during the entire war. Finding the staggering loss of ships

too high a cost for the total lack of return, the Grubs soon left the sytem alone.

After the war, the Bokchi kept a large portion of their new military and planned for the future. Within a few years, they had eradicated the Grubs from several neighboring systems and taken them for their own. The newly taken planets are currently undergoing terraforming, and will become food supply planets for the collective. Despite the hard times, the Bokchi still maintain a sizable presence in the Frontier and are, in the eyes of some of their lesser-defended neighbors, getting greedy.

## Homestead

**System:** KZ-24N9
**World:** Homestead
**Class:** Planet
**Natural Satellites:** None
**State:** N/Ap
**Status:** Independent
**Autonomy:** Full
**Evironment:** Farmland
**Habitat:** Normal
**Gravity:** 1.2
**Atmosphere:** Normal
**% H$_2$O:** 74
**Mean Temp** — 00 lat: s 90 / w 70
    450 lat: s 80 / w 30
**Diameter:** 8,400 km
**Axial Tilt:** 140
**Day:** 29.8 hours
**Year:** 374.2 days
**Danger:** None
**Race:** Homesteader
**Population:** 17 million
**Social Adaptations:**
**Trade:** Agriculture
**Government:** Democratic

**Notes:** Homestead was one of the few planets essentially passed over during the influx of the Night Brood. Having no military to speak of and nothing of real interest to the Grubs, the swarm didn't bother to make the short detour necessary to take the planet. Being outside of the battles going on through most of the rest of the Empire, the Homesteaders continued with their life much as they had before.

In the first years after the war, however, several factions deemed Homestead as a suitable place to inhabit. The Homesteaders had become accustomed to their isolation, and they resented the audacity of these newcomers to reap the benefits of the world the colonists had tamed. A decision was made to ban all mass immigration. Some factions tried to take the planet by force and were met by a small but determined fleet of starfighters. The Homesteaders successfully repelled several attempted invasions and have kept their world as their own ever since.

## Keota

**System:** Kernat
**World:** Keota
**Class:** Planet
**Natural Satellites:** None
**State:** Keotan Technologies, Inc.
**Status:** Alliance capitol
**Autonomy:** Full
**Evironment:** Natural
**Habitat:** Normal
**Gravity:** 1.3
**Atmosphere:** Thin
**% H$_2$O:** 35
**Mean Temp** — 00 lat: s 95 / w  80
    450 lat: s 70 / w  40
**Diameter:** 14,200 km
**Axial Tilt:** 80
**Day:** 18.6 hours
**Year:** 224.1 days
**Danger:** None
**Race:** Keotan
**Population:** 97 million
**Social Adaptations:** Highly technological
**Trade:** Technology
**Government:** Technocracy

**Notes:** Keota was one of the systems that barely survived the onslaught of the Night Brood. Originally encompassing a full system, the remains of the Keota Enclave have withdrawn onto the capitol world of Keota IV.

Having nothing of material worth in the system, the Keotans originally established themselves as a scientific enclave and began exporting ther knowledge to the rest of the Frontier and, on occasion, back towards the Core.

With the coming of the Grubs, the Keotans were sheared back to their capitol world. There, they made a final stand and, with heavy losses, maintained their hold on the planet.

Since the end of the war, they have begun to expand again, though tentatively, into the rest of the system. They have stayed clear of the planets for the time, and are instead carving out homes on the moons and asteroids of their system. One of their primary goals is the gathering of significant information on the Night Brood in an attempt to develop chemical or biological weapons capable of wiping them out while leaving the infested planets capapble of supporting human life. It is their intention to use this technology personally and claim the cleaned planets as their own.

Since the coming of the Prometheans, the Keotans have allied themselves with the Draconians. The technological exchanges between the two have been beneficial to both and appear to be nowhere near ending. Due to the small population, the Keotan society has placed large portions of its industry and defense in the hands of automated machinery. Though they are being sure to keep it small and independent enough to avoid the mistakes of ASP.

## Prague

**System:** Prague
**World:** Homeworld
**Class:** Moon
**Natural SatellitesS:** N/Ap
**State:** United Republic of Homeworld States ("Prague")
**Status:** Republic capitol
**Autonomy:** Full
**Evironment:** Harsh
**Habitat:** Normal
**Gravity:** 1.2
**Atmosphere:** Normal
**% H$_2$O:** 26
**Mean Temp** — 00 lat: s 90 / w  70
    450 lat: s 80 / w  40
**Diameter:** 7800  km
**Axial Tilt:** 80
**Day:** 76.5 hours
**Year:** 7658.4 days
**Race:** Pragan

time you talk about it, I'm almost able to see it a little more." She took her hand from his chest and let one finger gently trace the lines of age on his face. Only a small portion of the soft, tanned skin showed above the thick salt-and-pepper of his beard. "Do you think it's still there?"

"I don't know. I don't want to find out. I don't want to set foot on Barat-Tuul and see that all I had loved is laid waste. I don't want to know what they have done." He turned his head to look into her deep blue eyes. "That is for the young ones. The new generations. They have no memories of what it was; only dreams of what it could be." He closed his eyes as his chest rose again with a deep sigh. "Let the dreams do what the memories cannot."

**Population**: 3.5 billion
**Social Adaptations**: Harsh marxism
**Trade**: Mining
**Government**: Marxist dictatorship

**Notes**: Prague is a planet formerly falling under Bokchito's power, though often at odds with them on minor policy decisions. At the time of the War, the Bokchi government severed all ties when it was decided that Prague would be of little defensive value. The new government of Prague took the opportunity to establish itself quickly before the Hatchlings arrived. When the Grubs did reach the fringes of the Prague system, the residents were ready to defend themselves.

Having at one time been a major arms manufacturer for the Bokchito Collective, Prague was able to produce a large military machine quickly. The pilots and gunners were inexperienced, and a large number of them were killed, but the thought of surviving to independence from their Bokchi oppressors did much to spur the survivors on. After the last of the Grubs were repelled from the sysytem, the high-ranking fighters returned to grand victory parades and a lush lifestyle. The remainder of the populace, however, returned to the oppression of the new government.

Without the Bokchi to suppress them, the Prague government has begun a policy of expansion wherever possible. In the post-war Frontier, Prague has become a new and viable power.

## Rattan

**System**: KDP-989
**World**: Rattan
**Class**: Planet
**Natural Satellites**:
**State**: Confederated Rattanni States
**Status**: Federation Capitol
**Autonomy**: Full
**Evironment**: Natural
**Habitat**: Normal
**Gravity**: 1.6
**Atmosphere**: Normal
**% $H_2O$**: 54
**Mean Temp** — 00 lat: s 89 / w  69
　　　　450 lat: s 76/ w 38
**Diameter**: 14,700 km

**Axial Tilt**: 240
**Day**: 68.7 hours
**Year**: 669.5 days
**Race**: Rattan
**Population**: 12 billion
**Social Adaptations**:
**Trade**: Industry
**Government**: Dictatorship

**Notes**: Rattan was, at one time, the center of a miniature empire within the greater Terran Empire. With a strong and ruthless military, the Rattanni Government engulfed the many systems around it's homeworld, taking control of their military and economy, while granting very little in return. The one thing they did give, however, was peace. Battle between the worlds were eliminated, and the few internal uprisings were quickly quelled with an obvious show of force.

One of the edicts of the Rattanni government was a ban on all forms of birth control. Through this, they developed a large underclass which became a form of slave labor for the dominating capitol. Being careful to regulate the strength—both physical and mental—of its population, the Rattanni leaders avoided breeding a people capable of revolt.

When the Night Brood advanced on the worlds under Rattanni rule, the government armed it's subjects and sent them out as cannon fodder. Using the huge populations of the subjugated worlds to slow down the advancing horde, and sacrificing those worlds when it became convenient, the Rattanni were able to soften the strength of the Grubs. They finally sent out the main force of the Rattanni Navy and, fresh to the fight, wiped out the Grubs in just a few decisive battles.

Caring very little for the fate of the sacrificed worlds, the Rattanni quickly began looking for new worlds to advance upon and claim in the wake of the Night Brood advance. When the Prometheans came into the picture, the Rattanni soon allied themselves with the Draconian factions, feeling that the Primates were weak and not to be trusted. The brutal honesty of the Draconians in their claims of superiority appealed to the Rattanni.

With the help of the Draconians, the Rattannni have been able to carry out a slow but progressive advancement upon their neighbors.

## Taber

**System**: KDL-34NX5
**World**: Trask
**Class**: Planet
**Natural Satellites**:
**State**: N/Ap
**Status**: Independent state
**Autonomy**: Full
**Evironment**: Natural
**Habitat**: Natural
**Gravity**: 0.9
**Atmosphere**: Normal (O$_2$ rich)
**% H$_2$O**: 54
**Median Temp**— 00 lat: s 100/ w  80
        450 lat: s 90 / w  60
**Diameter** 8,400 km
**Axial Tilt:** 40
**Day:** 26.1 hours
**Year:** 358.5 days
**Danger:** None
 **Race**: Taban
**Population**: 2.4 million
**Social Adaptations**: None
**Trade**: Agriculture
**Government**: Loose bureaucracy

Notes: Trask is a highly contested agricultural planet falling midway between the boundaries of Argent and Taber. It has two main appeals for each side: its potential for food production and its location as an encroachment upon the other's territory. At present, Taber has a small defensive force occupying the planet, and has laid claim to it.

## Starcraft Point Cost Table

| Starcraft | Basic Point Value | Crew |
|---|---|---|
| Saucer Shuttle | 6 | 1 |
| Pit Viper | 12 | 1 |
| Wind Jammer | 13 | 1 |
| Borax 1000t Frieghter | 18 | 1 |
| Spirit Rider | 18 | 1 |
| Blizzard | 19 | 1 |
| Dart | 21 | 1 |
| Thunder Bird | 25 | 1 |
| Wave Cutter | 25 | 1 |
| Kosmos | 27 | 1 |
| Curtis Shuttle | 30 | 1 |
| Hell Bender | 32 | 1 |
| Talon | 33 | 1 |
| Shryak Shuttle | 34 | 2 |
| Blood Hawk | 41 | 1 |
| Teal Hawk | 43 | 2 |
| Night Hawk | 47 | 1 |
| Crescent | 55 | 3 |
| Death Wind | 60 | 2 |
| Lance Electra | 60 | 2 |
| Havok | 61 | 2 |
| Salamander | 66 | 2 |
| Sorenson III | 68 | 2 |
| Avenger | 78 | 2 |
| Sentry | 80 | 3 |
| Glaive | 106 | 2 |
| Epping | 119 | 4 |
| Revenge | 120 | 2 |
| Pharsii II | 120 | 3 |
| Seraph | 121 | 2 |
| Drakar | 121 | 5 |
| Scorpion | 122 | 4 |
| Star Raven | 125 | 4 |
| Spider | 129 | 3 |
| Catastrophe | 142 | 4 |
| Eagle | 170 | 5 |
| Conestoga | 215 | 5 |
| Betafortress | 216 | 5 |
| Betafortress Alpha | 218 | 6 |
| Betafortress Beta | 220 | 6 |

# New and Upcoming Products!

**St #7200    Silent Death: The Next Millennium™ Deluxe Box                    $50.00**

Here's everything you need for the complete *Silent Death* experience! The new Rulebook contains updated rules from the original *Silent Death* and the first edition supplement *Overkill™* and *Black Guard™*. A major new feature is the point-based ship design system that allows players to construct their own fighters. These ships and graphics have been comprehensively updated and improved. Throw in the two large hex sheets, 9 polyhedral dice, 48 plastic ships with bases, lots of plastic markers, an introductory scenario booklet, a ship display booklet, and you're ready to fly into battle!

**St #7201    Silent Death: The Next Millennium™ (Rulebook Only)                    $18.00**

**St #7210    Renegades: The Espan Rebellion™                    $12.00**

This first supplement for *SD:TNM*, describes the rebels' struggle to win their freedom once and for all. It features details about the Espan Civil War, including nearly 20 scenarios and a mini-campaign system, as well as starcraft displays for six new ships. It also introduces the use of tractor beams and salvage claws into *Silent Death* combat.

**St #7211    Sunrunners™                    MAR        $12.00**

With the end of the Terran-Hatchling War, the frontier is expanding once again. Force is often the first resource of the powerful and weak alike. *Sunrunners* reveals everything there is to know about the last survivors of Barat-Tuul, from their birth by fire to their nomadic warmongering. Includes rules for new weapons and six new ships.

**St #7410    Wings of Death™ (SD boxed miniatures)                    APRIL        $30.00**

This is a boxed set of 48 finely crafted plastic space fighters sculpted by Bob Naismith for our explosive *Silent Death™*! These are the same ships included in the *Silent Death: The Next Millennium™* Deluxe Box game, and include 4 each of 12 different ship designs. The ships are unfinished and can be painted with acrylic or enamel colors. They are also appropriate for any other space combat game or RPG. (Produced in conjunction with Hobbygames Ltd., U.K.)

**St #7611    Steel Warriors™ (boxed miniatures)                    $25.00**

This box contains six sprues, each with five robots and eleven mix-and-match weapon systems that fit any of the robots. Included are 2 large humanoid robots, 2 small humanoid robots, 1 mobile assault robot. The figures are unfinished and can be painted with acrylic or enamel colors so you can create your own unique *Steel Warriors* for a wide range of miniatures games! (Produced in conjunction with Hobbygames Ltd., U.K.)

**St #7612    Space Rangers™ (boxed miniatures)                    MAR        $25.00**

This boxed set contains 50 highly detailed, generic plastic miniatures with advanced weapons, back mounted jump packs and life support systems. Included are 10 Squad Leaders each armed with a hand laser and Power Sabre, and 40 Space Rangers, with personal weapons as well as 30 mix-and-match heavy weapons. These figures are unfinished and can be painted with enamel or acrylic colors. Suitable for a wide range of miniatures games. (Produced in conjunction with Hobbygames Ltd., U.K.)

**St #7212    Warhounds™                    APRIL        $14.00**

*Silent Death™* just keeps getting bigger. Until now, the *Silent Death* game has confined itself to starfighters and the slightly larger gunboats. *Warhounds* changes all of that, introducing escort-class ships into the *Silent Death* game for the first time. This 96-page book comes complete with starcraft displays for six new gigantic starcraft, plus rules for how to build your very own escorts using *Silent Death's* ship design system. Two-hex-long figures for each of the six new ships will be released by RAFM concurrently. Watch out for *Warhounds*. Believe us: you'd rather be with them than against them!

Iron Crown Enterprises, Inc.
P.O. Box 1605 Charlottesville, VA 22902
1(800) 325-0479
e-mail: vaice@aol.com
web page: http://www.ironcrown.com

Hobbygames, Ltd., U.K.
Unit S4, Rudford Industrial Estates
Ford Airfield, Near Arundel
West Sussex, UK BN18 0BD
1903 730998